A
MAGICAL
YEAR

ABOUT THE AUTHOR

Susanna Bailey is an artist who has exhibited nationally and internationally since leaving the Slade School of Fine Art. She has contributed to various journals and magazines, and writes alongside her own visual work.

ACKNOWLEDGEMENTS

I have collected these poems and sayings from a kaleidoscope of literary sources, from my father's weathered books, which we shared when I was little, to the breezy internet which now shouts all that can be seen and heard in every form and in every shape from time immemorial. No library or anthology, though, can claim the exclusive personal universe that words convey to every reader individually. Poems read to me as a child conjured up pictures which were just mine, and later I would use them to inspire my creative instincts. Words transmit signals, words take chances, and words create ideas.

I have to thank every ancient voice that placed their thoughts before me, and every modern writer who integrates their lives with mine to inspire and pave the way forward. I would like to thank my publisher Jo Lal, for her blind faith, my editors Steve Williamson and Jessica Cuthbert-Smith for their gentle nudging, Naseem Ashun for her insight, Penny Escombe, whose awesome memory for poetry and quotes has often reduced me to tears of laughter, The Revd Richard Coles for his kind and gentle nature, and support of this book, and my dog Stoker, who, albeit on only three legs, has walked me through my thoughts, and half way around the world.

A
MAGICAL
YEAR

Lift Your Spirit with 365 Poems and Reflections from Around the World

EDITED BY SUSANNA BAILEY

TRIGGER™
The mental health & wellbeing publisher

To little Élodie Grace, born in owl-light;
together, we will explore the darknesses
that can sometimes hide a world
drenched in sunshine. Together.

First published in Great Britain 2020 by Trigger
Trigger is a trading style of Shaw Callaghan Ltd & Shaw Callaghan 23
USA, INC.
The Foundation Centre
Navigation House, 48 Millgate, Newark
Nottinghamshire NG24 4TS UK
www.triggerpublishing.com

British Library Cataloguing in Publication Data
A CIP catalogue record for this book is available upon request
from the British Library

ISBN: 9781789562231
This book is also available in eBook format:
ePUB: 9781789562248

Cover design by Steve Williams Creative
Typeset by JCS Publishing Services Ltd
Printed and bound in Great Britain by CPI Group (UK) Ltd,
Croydon CRO 4YY
Paper from responsible sources

CONTENTS

FOREWORD

I write this six months into the Covid-19 pandemic, and like everyone else, I am looking back now and wondering how it has changed my life. I am relatively lucky. I am solvent, employed and have a nice vicarage in the country; but I was also widowed last Christmas, and that is a long, hard haul.

I have spent much more time in the garden. Watching things come and go, the turning cycle of the year, has helped me to grieve and to heal. The dogs have never been so diligently and tirelessly walked, I have rediscovered the joys of cycling and lost more than a stone; and I have rediscovered the joys of cooking, which threatens to put it back on.

And I have read a lot more poetry. I have always loved poetry, after being required to learn it by heart as a little boy, before I knew such things were a chore. I was a chorister too, and grew up steeped in the poetry of the Psalms and the language of the King James Bible and the Book of Common Prayer. It has not only stayed with me; I realize now it has formed me: my outlook, my character, my way of understanding the world. Now, pushing sixty, I find rhyming couplets, verses and sometimes whole poems, leaping into my mind.

During full lockdown I lost the ability to read fiction, or anything long. Perhaps I was distracted by the challenges of this time, perhaps it was grief, perhaps both. Poetry came to the rescue, giving strength, consolation and challenge … a treasury of reflection from across the world and down the ages, which has enabled me to stand up and face forward. … And, more than that, to discover that delight, fascination nd stimulation are still there, waiting for me to be ready to perience them again.

May it do the same for you.

The Revd Richard Coles

INTRODUCTION

A book of poems is like a bowl of cherries, or a chalice filled up to the brim with wine. Throughout history we have always told each other stories that will nourish our imagination and soothe our fears – just as, when there are no other words to be found, we can offer a small cup or bowl of food to a stranger in an act of fellowship.

Early in the 15th century, poetry became the most popular form of entertainment for princes and paupers alike. It was often seen as a cure for fear or sorrow, and people were encouraged to listen to a bard reciting "joyful and strange things", as prescribed by Aldobrandino of Siena in his treatise, *Régime du Corps*.

Poetry is found within language. Words and sounds, forged into patterns or rhythms, can be set in memory and repeated aloud. Poetry can be traced back to the inscriptions carved into cave walls and it flows like an endless torrent throughout time. It has long been a sanctuary for mankind's most intimate thoughts; many of us can remember a few lines or have written some ourselves in times of need or enlightenment. These lines often begin as a private notion, scribbled down, and, as often as not, will go no further. However, some are listened to, remembered and recorded. They stand the test of time, and are learned by later generations. Other poems were folded into long stories like the Old Testament or Shakespeare's works, while yet others would become the fabric of folklore, and others simple nursery rhymes.

Every culture has had a story about its inception, memorialized in countless poems about a pure land left behind in the wake of mankind's greed and enmity. Power has been eulogized in epic poems; sadness in the great tragedies; love fuels the greatest epiphanies; the gods are found in prayer, and death in a requiem.

Tales of transformation and hope, both real and fictional, can come together and raise us to a higher state of being. They are the way that we attempt to balance the paradoxes of life: fragility and strength; success and failure; the logical and the irrational; ignorance and understanding; life and death.

A poem can call you to look deeper into yourself and can guide you in times of darkness. Carefully crafted words can refresh your perceptions and revive a lasting hope in times of distress. They can make you laugh and they can make you cry. Poetry is an ancient and esoteric form of giving, of taking, of sharing. Just like a bowl filled with nourishment, a book can nurture the subconscious as much as the conscious; it can soothe a broken heart, spark ideas, quench the bitter taste of loneliness, awaken the spirit or simply make you smile. A poem has the power to unleash your imagination and to hold you back from the brink of despair. It can cast a spell or perform extraordinary transformative magic in the space of a single moment.

This collection has been gathered from fragments of the past and selected from many cultures. The poems, thoughts and reflections have been brought together to foster a renewed sense of wellbeing and they invite you to touch upon the wisdom of your inner self and tap into the knowledge handed down in the echoes of our ancestors.

There are 365 poems and quotes in this collection, divided into eight special parts which follow the seasons and celebrate the most important things in life: Beginnings and winter; Purification and Awakening follow on through spring; summer brings Growth and Prosperity; autumn comes with Harmony and Gratitude; Endings completes the full cycle, ready for new beginnings again. Choose from any of these titles, study one in particular or follow the year through the seasons. You can read it from beginning to end one day at a time or you can dip into it whenever or wherever you like. You might sample any poem or lines from the book for breakfast, or at midday, or just before you turn off the light. Poetry is known to heal and calm, to distract and awaken, but more than anything it helps you to understand the world around you and ultimately yourself.

Take this book as you would perhaps accept a bowl full of fresh fruit from the hands of a stranger or a friend. Let it nourish you and strengthen you as you set out on another twenty-four hours of a brand-new day.

1

I quote others only in order
the better to express myself.

Michel de Montaigne,
French Renaissance philosopher and essayist,
1533–1592

BEGINNINGS
WINTER–SPRING

Would you be ready to accept that, at any given moment, something significant could be about to happen? Something special might be going to take place that changes the entire course of your life – it could be the birth of a baby or it might be a much smaller event, a stroke of luck or a seemingly predestined act of fate.

To start anything takes courage and caution, all at the same time. Maybe you have just fallen in love, or perhaps you have realized that the opposite has happened.

Are you leaving something or someone behind to set off on a new phase of your life? Are you beginning anew?

Our bodies renew cells over and over again in split seconds, and our minds process unimaginable amounts of information every day, simply so that we are able to begin a new cycle, or to step out of bed in the morning.

Could this beginning be the first time you have actually listened to your inner voice or concentrated deeply on the words spoken by another? Beginnings sometimes require endings and bravery; they can be dependent on forgiveness and may need care; they may spring out of innocence, or we might need purification or absolution before progressing. They may appear joyous, or might rely on redemption. Beginnings can be as simple as clearing out a cupboard or recycling the rubbish.

There are philosophies devoted to proving that there are no beginnings and no endings, only what exists in the present moment. There are religions that are defined by the nature of both a beginning and an end.

More often than not, a beginning can be as uncomplicated as opening a book that will lead you to new places full of transformation and wisdom. Since time began, we have found sustenance in other people's words. There have always been first steps, or moments when we metaphorically set sail into the future. It is never too late to venture forth out on a beginning.

QUESTIONS TO REFLECT ON

Before you start on this book of poetry and wisdom, take a moment to pause and ask yourself what the word "beginning" means to you.

- ❖ If you are starting something new, have you thought about why?

- ❖ Is this the right time to take the first step on a new beginning?

- ❖ Is everything in place for the processes of transformation to unfold positively?

- ❖ Will the steps that you take involve the people around you? Will they be safe as you move on?

When starting afresh you will need time, and resolve, to try out new ideas. Things may not be quite how you want them to be, so be willing to change, knowing that nothing stays the same as time moves on. Remember to ask questions, and listen carefully to the answers. Don't worry if you lose sight of the objective on the way (a poet would say that this was probably meant to be), and don't be afraid if your plans seem to go astray. There is always another way.

A beginning starts with a journey, and it is the journey, not the goal, that is the most important thing. Enjoy.

2

O reader! Had you in your
  mind
Such stories as silent thought
  can bring,
O gentle reader! You can find
A tale in every thing.

William Wordsworth,
English Romantic poet,
1770–1850

3

It is never too late to be what you might have been.

George Eliot, pen name of Mary Ann Evans,
English novelist, poet, journalist and translator,
1819–1880

4

The hazel-blooms, in threads of crimson hue,
Peep through the swelling buds, foretelling Spring,
Ere yet a white-thorn leaf appears in view,
Or March finds throstles pleased enough to sing.
To old touchwood tree woodpeckers cling
A moment, and their harsh-toned notes renew;
In happier mood, the stockdove claps his wing;
The squirrel sputters up the powdered oak,
With tail cocked o'er his head, and ears erect,
Startled to hear the woodman's understroke;
And with the courage which he fears collect,
He hisses fierce half malice and half glee –
Leaping from branch to branch about the tree,
In winters foliage, moss and lichens, drest.

John Clare,
English poet,
1793–1864
"First Sight of Spring"

5

There is no Frigate like a Book
To take us Lands away.
Nor any Coursers like a Page
Of prancing Poetry –
This Travel may the poorest take
Without offence of Toll –
How frugal is the Chariot
That bears the Human Soul –

Emily Dickinson,
American poet,
1830–1886
"There Is No Frigate Like a Book"

6

Take time to work, it is the price of success.
Take time to think, it is the source of power.
Take time to play, it is the secret of perpetual
   youth.
Take time to read, it is the fountain of wisdom.
Take time to be friendly, it is the road to happiness.
Take time to dream, it is hitching your wagon to a
   star.
Take time to look around, it is too short a day to be
   selfish.
Take time to laugh, it is the music of the soul.

Anonymous,
Old English prayer

7

My bird, the struggle's over!
Thy wings, at length unfurled,
Will bear thee, noble rover,
Through yon blue, airy world.

Thy fearless breast has shaken
Earth's dust and dew away;
Thine eye it's aim has taken –
Its mark the orb of day.

Then, as an eagle training
Her tender young to fly,
The hand, that's all sustaining,
Will lift thee to the sky.

While higher, higher soaring
Thou'lt feel thy cares are drowned
Where heaven's bright SUN is pouring
A flood of glory round.

Hannah Flagg Gould,
American poet,
1789–1865
From "The Rising Eagle"

8

Apple orchards, the trees all cover'd
   with blossoms,
Wheat fields carpeted far and near in
   vital emerald green;
The eternal, exhaustless freshness of
   each early morning,
The yellow, golden, transparent haze of
   the warm afternoon sun;
The aspiring lilac bushes with profuse
   purple or white flowers.

Walt Whitman,
American poet, journalist and essayist,
1819–1892
"Out of May's Shows Selected"

9

The place you are right now
God circled on a map for you.

Hafez,
Persian poet and philosopher,
1315–1390

10

Awake! for the Morning in the
  bowl of night
Has flung the stone that puts
  the stars to flight:
And lo! the Hunter of the East
  has caught
The Sultans turret in a noose
  of light.

Edward Fitzgerald,
English poet and translator,
1809–1883
From *The Rubaiyat of Omar Khayyam*

11

A journey of a thousand miles begins with a single step.

Lao Tzu,
Chinese philosopher and writer,
6th/4th century BCE

12

The beginning is the most important part of the work.

Plato,
Greek philosopher,
428–347 BCE

13

If you were not a star I would be in the dark.

Hafsa bint al-Hajj Arrakuniyya,
Andalusian poet,
1135–1190

14

It is so small a thing
To have enjoy'd the sun,
To have lived light in the
  spring,
To have loved, to have
  thought, to have done …?

Matthew Arnold,
English poet,
1822–1888
The Hymn of Empedocles

15

Om Shanti, Shanti, Shanti

("Om" is a Sanskrit sound that invokes
greeting, and "Shanti" means "peace".
It brings peace to the physical, the
spiritual and the mental realms.
It can be repeated over and
over again as an offering.)

16

"I have no name
I am but two days old."
What shall I call thee?
"I happy am,
Joy is my name."
Sweet joy befall thee!

Pretty joy!
Sweet joy but two days old,
Sweet joy I call thee:
Thou dost smile,
I sing the while,
Sweet Joy befall thee!

William Blake,
English poet, painter and printmaker,
1757–1827
"Infant Joy"

17

The beginning is always today.

Mary Wollstonecraft Shelley,
English writer and philosopher,
1797–1851

18

May you always have enough
  happiness to keep you sweet,
Enough trials to keep you strong,
Enough success to keep you eager,
Enough faith to give you courage,
And enough determination to make
  each day a good day.

**Anonymous,
blessing**

19

Every new beginning comes from some other beginning's end.

Seneca,
Roman Stoic philosopher,
4 BCE–65 CE

20

Making the beginning is one third of the work.

Irish proverb

21

We are made from Mother Earth and we go back to Mother Earth.

Shenandoah,
Oneida chief,
1706–1816,
Native American proverb

22

Every day is a fresh beginning,
Listen my soul to the glad refrain.
And, spite of old sorrows
And old sinning,
Troubles forecasted
And possible pain,
Take heart with the day and begin
again.

Susan Coolidge,
pen name of Sarah Chauncey Woolsey,
American children's author,
1835–1905
"New Every Morning"

23

Blossom by blossom the spring begins.

Algernon Charles Swinburne,
English poet and playwright,
1837–1909

24

Spring unlocks the flowers to paint the laughing soil.

Bishop Reginald Heber,
poet and hymn-writer,
1783–1826

25

Bloom where you are planted.

New Testament, 1 Corinthians 7.20–24

26

Bliss was it in the dawn to be
  alive,
But to be young was very
  heaven!

William Wordsworth,
English Romantic poet,
1770–1850
From "The French Revolution, as it Appeared
to Enthusiasts at its Commencement"

27

Spring is the time for plans and projects.

Leo Tolstoy,
Russian author,
1828–1910

28

A kind word is like a Spring Day.

Russian proverb

29

No matter how hard the past is, you can always begin again.

Gautama Buddha,
philosopher, spiritual teacher and religious leader,
5th–4th century BCE

30

Everyone wants happiness
No one wants pain,
But you can't have a rainbow
Without a little rain.

Anonymous

31

We are all travellers in this
wilderness of the world
And the best we can find
in our travels is an honest
friend.

Robert Louis Stevenson,
Scottish novelist, poet and travel writer,
1850–1894

32

Be careful what you wish for,
lest it come true.

Aesop,
Greek fabulist and storyteller,
c.620–564 BCE
From *Aesop's Fables*

33

As my eyes search the prairie
I feel the summer in the spring

Frances Densmore (translator)
"Chippewa" ("Dream Song") (Native American)

34

My soul is awakened, my spirit
is soaring
And carried aloft on the
wings of the breeze;
From above and around me
the wild wind is roaring,
Arousing to rapture the
earth and the seas.

Anne Brontë,
English novelist and poet,
1820–1849
From "Lines Composed in a Wood on a Windy Day"

35

You who want
Knowledge,
Seek the Oneness
Within
There you
will find
the clear mirror
already waiting.

Hadewijch of Antwerp,
Belgian poet and mystic,
1200–1248
"You Who Want"
trans. Joseph Van Mierlo (d.1823), Netherlands

36

"Hope" is a thing with
 feathers –
That perches in the soul –
And sings the tune without
 the words –
And never stops – at all –

Emily Dickinson,
American poet,
1830–1886
From "'Hope' Is a Thing With Feathers"

37

Bless us oh Lord
For these, thy gifts,
Which we are about to receive
May the Lord make us truly
  grateful.

From *Book of Common Prayer*

38

To dry one's eyes and laugh at
  a fall,
And, baffelled, get up and
  begin again.

Robert Browning,
English poet and playwright,
1812–1889

39

"Where shall I begin, please your Majesty?" he asked. "Begin at the beginning," the King said, gravely, "and go on 'til you come to the end: then stop."

Lewis Carroll,
English writer,
1832–1898
From *Alice in Wonderland*

40

By viewing Nature, Nature's
handmaid Art,
Makes mighty things from
small beginnings grow:
Thus fishes first to shipping
did impart,
Their tail the rudder, and
their head the prow.

John Dryden,
English literary critic, translator,
playwright and first Poet Laureate,
1631–1700
From "Annus Mirabilis"

41

'Tis not necessary to light a candle to the sun.

Algernon Sidney,
English politician,
1623–1683
From *Discourses on Government*

42

The most glorious moments in your life are not the so-called days of success, but rather those days when out of dejection and despair you feel rise in you a challenge to life, and the promise of future accomplishments.

Gustave Flaubert,
French novelist,
1821–1880
trans. Eleanor Marx Aveling, 1886

43

Take only memories, leave
nothing but footprints.

Native American proverb

44

Start a huge, foolish project,
   like Noah …
It makes absolutely no
   difference
What people think of you.

Rumi,
Persian poet and mystic,
1207–1273

45

In creating, the only hard thing
  is to begin;
A grass blade's no easier to
  make then an oak.

James Russell Lowell,
American poet,
1819–1891

PURIFICATION
SPRING

When asked what was meant by purity, the Prophet Muhammad described a place where the heart was pure from all sin, meaning a state where the heart was free from envy, pride and hatred. To support this idea physical cleanliness must also be observed throughout the daily lives of all who believe in Islam.

Many religions and cultures share this simple belief, that our lives are healthier and our spirits stronger if we can maintain a life of inner purity and outer cleanliness. The great religions are punctuated with symbolic stories about "washing away the sins of the world", of baptizing, immersing in water and ceremonies of initiation into a higher, purer state of being. Purity is a desire that many people share during their lives, and a concept that guides our humanity with wellbeing and kindness.

In order to achieve a better way "to be", it is important to seek out the stories that broaden our understanding of purification. Clarity is a type of purity and is imperative when we're attempting to interpret an idea or comprehend the reason for something. The right words, lucidity, even appropriate actions, can help to free something from indistinctness or ambiguity. An example of this can be seen in nature. Winter quietly magics away the debris of the past year by absorbing the rotting leaves, mulching them in with the spring rains and drawing them down into the soil. In this way the new growth has a clear space to grow into and the surface of the ground is cleansed. Through natural processes, a clarity has been born out of clutter.

Sometimes purification can be construed as a form of honesty if by that we mean that there is no corruption within an idea. Here honesty is more of a policy than an action. Honesty and truth are often held to be the better way to behave in order to achieve high moral standards. As normal people, we often need reminding about this because the temptations to behave in an uncivilized manner can be very seductive. Mark Twain enjoyed playing with the ideas pertaining to honesty, saying simple things like, "When in doubt, tell the truth."

As we think about purification there is an old maxim about a bowl of muddy liquid. It symbolizes a muddled assortment of thoughts and emotions that together discolour the water. Fragments of lies and particles of anger swill about, staining the inner surface of the bowl. They only disappear when the water is still and everything has sunk and has settled on the bottom of the vessel. The water is now genuinely clear and transparent. Why then, the maxim goes, when everything is crystal clear– why then take a stick to it, and stir it all up again?

Purification leads to wonderful new things; it renews, it enhances and it helps us to find a better self. It erases confusion and restores peace; it is a powerful force that can transform the psyche, just as it can clear and refresh the earth, and ready it for another year.

QUESTIONS TO REFLECT ON

The act of purification begins when we can take some time to look gently, deeply into our inner self and ask questions worded with clarity and honesty.

❖ How well do I know myself?

❖ From a more existential angle, who does honesty benefit most, what or who is really authentic? Could purity exist without honesty, transparency and clarity? How important are these things to you?

❖ How often, by returning to a negative thought or emotion, do you stir everything up again, and then regret the consequences?

❖ Are you happier when you are trying to be a "better person", both inwardly and outwardly?

Ultimately we should see that purification is part of a process and must not be mistaken for a cure or an ultimate goal.

It is never too late to transform your life through purification, clarity and honesty. You deserve to let your better self shine.

46

Awaiting snow,
Poets in their cups
See lightning flash.

Matsuo Bashō,
Japanese poet,
1644–1694

47

Aya!
Ayaya, it is beautiful it is out-doors when the summer
   comes at last.
Ayaya, ayaya, aya!

Ayaya, it is beautiful it is out-doors when the reindeer
   begin to come.
Ayaya, ayaya, aya!

Ayaya, when the roaring river rushes from the hills in
   summer.
Ayaya, ayaya, aya!

Ayaya, there is no reason to be mournful when the gulls
   cease crying.
Ayaya, ayaya, aya!

Ayaya, plenty of meat I shall have and plenty codfish.
Ayaya, ayaya, aya!

Ayaya, it is beautiful, beautiful it is out-doors when the
   summer comes at last.
Ayaya, ayaya, aya!

Franz Boas (translator),
American anthropologist,
1858–1942
"Summer Song" (Eskimo)

48

Oh! Come and breathe upon this fainting earth
Coolness and life. Is it that in his caves
He hears me? See, on yonder woody ridge,
The pine is bending his proud top, and now,
Among the nearer groves, chestnut and oak
Are tossing their green boughs about. He comes!
Lo, where the grassy meadow runs in waves!
The deep distressful silence of the scene
Breaks up the mingling of unnumbered sounds
And universal motion. He is come,
Shaking a shower of blossoms from the shrubs,
And bearing on their fragrance; and he brings
Music of birds, and rustling of young boughs,
And sound of swaying branches, and the voice
Of distant waterfalls. All the green herbs
Are stirring in his breath; a thousand flowers,
By the road-side and the borders of the brook,
Nod gaily to each other; glossy leaves
Are twinkling in the sun, as if the dew
Were on them yet, and silver waters break
Into small waves and sparkle as he comes.

William Cullen Bryant,
American Romantic poet and journalist,
1794–1878
"Summer Wind"

49

And it is you, spirit – with will and energy, and virtue and purity – that I want …

Charlotte Brontë,
English novelist and poet,
1816–1855
From *Jane Eyre*

50

Purity or impurity depends on oneself, no one can purify another.

Gautama Buddha,
philosopher, spiritual teacher and religious leader,
5th–4th century BCE

51

There's much afoot in heaven and earth this year;
The winds hunt up the sun, hunt up the moon,
Trouble the dubious dawn, hasten the drear
Height of a threatening moon.

No breath of boughs, no breath of leaves,
   of fronds,
May linger or grow warm; the trees are loud;
The forest, rooted, tosses in her bonds,
And strains against the cloud.

No scents may pause within the garden-fold;
The rifled flowers are cold as ocean-shells;
Bees, humming in the storm, carry their cold
Wild honey to cold cells.

Alice Meynell,
English writer and suffragist,
1847–1922
"The Rainy Summer"

52

Purity of soul cannot be lost without consent.

Saint Augustine,
Roman African theologian and philosopher,
354–430 CE

53

In the waters of purity, I melted like salt
Neither blasphemy, nor faith, nor
  conviction, nor doubt remained.
In the center of my heart a star has
  appeared
And all the seven heavens have
  become lost in it.

Rumi,
Persian poet and mystic,
1207–1273
"In the Waters of Purity"

54

The purest and most thoughtful minds are those which love colour the most.

John Ruskin,
English art critic and philosopher,
1819–1900
From *The Stones of Venice*

55

The light of love, the purity of
   grace,
The mind, the Music breathing
   from her face,
The heart whose softness
   harmonised the whole –
And, oh! That eye was in itself
   a Soul.

Lord Byron,
English poet,
1788–1824

56

I wish I could wash from our hearts and
  our souls
The stains of the week away,
And let water and air by their magic
  make
Ourselves as pure as they;
Then on the earth there would be
  indeed
A glorious washing day.

Louise May Alcott,
American novelist and poet,
1832–1888
From *Little Women*

57

Blessed be the pure of heart,
for they shall see God.

New Testament, Matthew 5:8

58

Can human folly harbour a more arrogant or ungrateful thought than the notion that whereas God makes man beautiful in body, man makes himself pure of heart.

Saint Augustine,
Roman African theologian
and philosopher,
354–430 CE
From *Selected Letters*

59

Purity of heart and clarity
of mind gives the surety
for life …

Anonymous

60

To the pure, all things are pure.

Marcel Proust,
French novelist,
1871–1922

61

God prefers bad verses recited
with a pure heart to the finest
verses chanted by the wicked.

Voltaire,
French Enlightenment writer,
1694–1778

62

Whoever tells a lie is not pure of heart, and such a person can not cook a clean soup.

Ludwig van Beethoven,
German composer,
1770–1827

63

O pure deep love, be here, be now,
Be always.
Worlds disappear in the tumult of
   samsara and neurotic thought,
And we frail leaves burn brighter with
   you then the cold stars.
Make me your core, your breath, your
   spirit.

Buddhist prayer

64

Mirroring each other:
white narcissi,
paper screen.

Matsuo Bashō,
Japanese poet,
1644–1694

65

The Moor is of a free and open
 nature,
That thinks men honest that
 but seem to be so.

William Shakespeare,
English playwright,
1564–1616
From *Othello*, Act I Scene 3

66

Purity is the feminine, Truth the masculine, of Honour.

Augustus William Hare,
English writer and historian,
1792–1834
From *Guesses at Truth*

67

Oh woman! Lovely woman! Nature
   made thee
To temper man: we had been brutes
   without you;
Angels are painted fair, to look like you;
There's in you all that we believe of
   heav'n,
Amazing brightness, purity, and truth,
Eternal joy, and everlasting love.

Thomas Otway,
English dramatist,
1652–1685
From *Venice Preserved*

68

To make your Children capable of honesty is the beginning of education.

John Ruskin,
English art critic and philosopher,
1819–1900

69

Honesty is the best policy.

William Shakespeare,
English playwright,
1564–1616

70

I eat my peas with honey,
I've done so all my life,
They do taste kind of funny,
But it keeps them on my knife.

Anonymous

71

Treat those who are good with
   goodness, and
Also treat those who are not good with
   goodness.
Thus goodness is attained.
Be honest to those who are honest, and
   be also
Honest to those who are not honest.
Thus honesty is attained.

Lao Tzu,
Chinese philosopher and writer,
6th/4th century BCE
trans. Thomas Wade, 1868

72

Confidence in others "honesty" is no light testimony of one's own integrity.

Michel de Montaigne,
French Renaissance philosopher and essayist,
1533–1592

73

Honesty is the best policy –
when there is money in it.

Mark Twain,
American writer and novelist,
1835–1910

74

If you want to know the end,
look at the beginning.
No matter how long the night,
the day is sure to come.

African proverb

75

Honest people don't hide their deeds.

Emily Brontë,
English novelist and poet,
1818–1848

76

Always tell the truth. That way you don't have to remember what you said.

Mark Twain,
American writer and novelist,
1835–1910

77

Be true to your work, your word, and your friend.

Henry David Thoreau,
American philosopher, essayist and poet,
1817–1862

78

Pictures of perfection, as you know make me sick and wicked.

Jane Austen,
English novelist,
1775–1817
From letter to Fanny Knight, *Pride and Prejudice*

79

Don't let anyone look down on you because you are young, but set an example for the believers in speech, in conduct, in love and in purity.

New Testament, 1 Timothy 4:12

80

Create for me a clean heart, O God and renew a right spirit within me.

Old Testament, Psalm 51:10

81

Your soul sees your perfection.

Rumi,
Persian poet and mystic,
1207–1273

82

O Mother race! to thee I bring
This pledge of faith unwavering,
This tribute to thy glory.
I know the pangs which thou didst feel,
When Slavery crushed thee wit its heel,
With thy dear blood all gory.

Thou hast the right to noble pride,
Whose spotless robes were purified
By blood's severe baptism.
Upon thy brow the cross was laid,
And labour's painful sweat-beads made
A consecrating chrism.

No other race, or white or black,
When bound as thou wert, to the rack,
So seldom stooped to grieving;
No other race, when free again,
Forgot the past and proved them men
So noble in forgiving.

Paul Lawrence Dunbar,
African-American poet,
1872–1906
From "Ode to Ethiopea"

83

But if he does really think that there is no distinction between virtue and vice, why, Sir, when he leaves our houses, let us count our spoons.

Samuel Johnson,
English writer,
1709–1784

84

I and my white cat Pangur
Each has his special art;
His mind is set on hunting mice
Mine on my special craft.

Better then fame I love to rest
With close study of my little book;
White Pangur does not envy me,
He loves to ply his childish art.

When we two are alone in our house
It is a tale without tedium;
Each of us has games never ending
Something to sharpen our wit upon.

At times by feats of valour
A mouse sticks in his net,
While in my net there drops
A loved law of obscure meaning.

His eye, this flashing full one,
He points against the fence wall

While against the fine edge of science,
I point my clear but feeble eye.

He is joyous with swift jumping
When a mouse sticks in his sharp claw,
And I too am joyous when I have grasped
The elusive but well loved problem.

Though we thus play at all times
Neither hinders the other –
Each is happy with his own art,
Pursues it with delight.

He is master of the work
Which he does every day
While I am master of my work
Bringing to obscure laws clarity.

Anonymous, 8th/9th-century marginal
poem on Codex S Pauli,
"The Monk and His Pet Cat, Pangur Bán"

85

A philosopher once asked
the Buddha: "Without words,
without the wordless, will you
tell me the truth?"
The Buddha kept silent.

Buddhist gatha

86

When I heard the learn'd astronomer,
When the proofs, the figures, were ranged in
   columns before me,
When I was shown the charts and diagrams, to
   add, divide, and measure them,
When I sitting heard the astronomer where
   he lectured with much applause in the
   lecture room.
When soon unaccountable I became tired
   and sick,
Till rising and gliding out I wander'd off by myself,
In the mystical moist night air, and from time
   to time,
Looked up in perfect silence at the stars.

Walt Whitman,
American poet, journalist and essayist,
1819–1892
"When I Heard the Learn'd Astronomer"

87

Be honest and true, boys,
Whatever you do, boys,
Let this be the motto through
   life.

George Birdseye,
American lyricist,
1844–1919

88

Once there was a little boy,
With curly hair and pleasant eye –
A boy who always told the truth,
And never, never, told a lie.

And when he trotted off to school,
The children all about would cry,
"There goes the curly-headed boy –
The boy that never tells a lie."

Anonymous
"The Boy Who Never Told a Lie"

89

I can resist everything except temptation.

Oscar Wilde,
Irish novelist and playwright,
1854–1900
From *Lady Windermere's Fan*

90

The louder they talked of his honour, the faster we counted our spoons.

Ralph Waldo Emerson,
American essayist and poet,
1803–1882

91

Do not pursue the past.
Do not lose yourself in the future.
The past no longer is.
The future has yet to come.
Looking deeply at life as it is
In the very here and now,
The practitioner dwells
In stability and freedom.

Buddhist teaching

92

Man cannot discover new oceans unless he has the courage to lose sight of the shore.

André Gide,
French author,
1869–1947

93

Life is a series of natural and
spontaneous changes.
Don't resist them; that only
creates sorrow. Let reality be
reality.
Let things flow naturally
forward in whatever way
they like.

Lao Tzu,
Chinese philosopher and writer,
6th/4th century BCE
trans. Thomas Wade, mid-19th century

94

Everything that is made beautiful and fair and lovely is made for the eye of one who sees.

Rumi,
Persian poet and mystic,
1207–1273

95

True life is lived when tiny changes occur.

Leo Tolstoy,
Russian author,
1828–1910

96

Dripping water hollows out stone, not through force but through persistence.

Ovid,
Roman poet,
43 BCE–17 CE

97

Only the wisest and stupidest of men never change.

Confucius,
Chinese philosopher,
551–479 BCE

AWAKENING
SPRING–SUMMER

Our cosmos is continually moving. While this green, white and blue planet rotates around a yellow sun, the seasons move in stages of constant renewal. Rivers that run dry during the summer revive and flow again when the snow melts and the rain falls; birds migrate thousands of miles, navigating the world, most often at night; and a rainbow can take your breath away just before it disappears. Nothing ever stays the same because almost everything we understand is changing right before our eyes. The one constant in our lives is that a continuum of impermanence spurs every moment into being; stillness often goes unnoticed.

Today there is not much time simply to sit and think, or just daydream, because "life must go on". We might wistfully long for things to go back to being the way they were, or want to be that child again who saw the world with eyes of innocence, or to go back to the moment when we first fell in love, or to find a love that has sadly disappeared from sight.

Throughout time, poetry has been one of the great therapies for anyone whose hopes and dreams need to be revived or reawakened and whose wellbeing depends on renewal and freshening. Poets have often undertaken a responsibility of care for the human spirit. Their role can be cathartic and curative. By sharing their most intimate thoughts and unveiling their emotions, they remind us that we are not alone. A poem can make sense of a moment – your moment – and reflect your innermost feelings and experiences. In this far-from-perfect world their words can be healing and improve our mental stability.

While the cosmos is one of constant motion, our minds are often in continual commotion. The literary effects of words and sound, visual imagery, metaphor and symbolism form a magnificent engine that can move us on to a heightened awareness and can be thought-provoking in times of need. In a few lines you might find that missing part of you lying hidden in a poet's hand.

The time that it takes to read a poem is a way of stepping out from the present moment into another dimension, into another world. This can feel like a magical "stillness", a calm, which may lead to a new awakening, or a new understanding or view of life. It's that moment when, metaphorically, the brakes are released and soundlessly the train slips out of the station. The journey has begun and you have left the past behind, while, for just a few seconds, you are suspended in time and space.

QUESTIONS TO REFLECT ON

❖ Are you aware how time just flies?

❖ Can you find a moment to daydream?

❖ What is it that makes you feel good about yourself?

❖ What is beautiful to you?

The ways to revive a drooping spirit are myriad, and every culture may differ, but there are universal methods of reawakening the spirit and touching joy again. Relax by listening to your favourite music and dance secretly to the sounds.

Step out into the air and breathe in deliberately. Watch yourself exhale. If you repeat this a few times you realize how alive you are at that very moment. Try to listen to others in a new way, without criticism, and read the tone of their voice instead of the words.

Julian of Norwich said in the 14th century, "All shall be well, and all shall be well, and all manner of things shall be well." She was an anchorite in the Middle Ages, and her book, *Revelations of Divine Love*, is the earliest surviving book in the English language written by a woman. She and her beloved cat would sit happily for hours in the abbey garden wrapped in deep contemplation and reverie.

It is an uplifting thought, and one to remember.

98

Into the scented woods we'll go,
And see the blackthorn swim with snow.
High above, in the budding leaves,
A brooding dove awakes and grieves;
The glades with mingled music stir,
And wildly laughs the woodpecker.
When blackthorn petals pearl the breeze,
There are the twisted hawthorn trees
Thick-set with buds, as clear and pale,
As golden water or green hail –
As if a storm of rain had stood
Enchanted in the thorny wood,
And, hearing fairy voices call,
Hung poised, forgetting how to fall.

Mary Webb,
English Romantic novelist and poet,
1881–1927
"Green Rain"

99

When I let go of what I am
I become what I might be.

Lao Tzu,
Chinese philosopher and writer,
6th/4th century BCE

100

There are some things that
one can only achieve by a leap
in the opposite direction.

Franz Kafka,
Czech novelist,
1883–1924

101

We must always change, renew, rejuvenate ourselves; otherwise, we harden.

Johann Wolfgang von Goethe,
German writer, philosopher and poet,
1749–1832

102

Awakening begins when a man realizes that he is going nowhere and does not know where to go.

G. I. Gurdjieff,
Armenian mystic and writer,
1886–1949

103

The greatest privilege of a life is to become a midwife to the awakening of the Soul in another person.

Plato,
Greek philosopher,
428–347 BCE

104

Spiritual awakening is the most essential thing in man's life, and it is the sole purpose of being. Is not civilization, in all its tragic forms, a supreme motive for spiritual awakening?

Khalil Gibran,
Lebanese-American writer and poet,
1883–1931

105

A single event can awaken within us a stranger totally unknown to us. To live is to be slowly born.

Antoine de Saint-Exupéry,
French writer and poet,
1900–1944

106

Carpe diem, quam minimum credula.

Seize the day, put no trust in the future.

Horace,
Roman lyric poet,
65 BCE–8 BCE

107

You have no need to travel anywhere – journey within yourself, enter a mine of rubies and bathe in the splendour of your own light.

Rumi,
Persian poet and mystic,
1207–1273

108

Festina lente.
Make haste slowly.

Augustus,
first Roman emperor,
63 BCE–14 CE

109

I have been happy tho' in a dream.
I have been happy – and I love the
theme:
Dreams! in their vivid colouring of life,
As in that fleeting, shadowy, misty strife
Of semblance with reality, which brings
To the delirious eye, more lovely things
Of Paradise and Love – and all our own!
Than young Hope in his sunniest hour
hath known.

Edgar Allen Poe,
American writer and poet,
1809–1849
From "Dreams"

110

Wherever you go, go with all your heart.

Confucius,
Chinese philosopher,
551–479 BCE

111

This is the weather the cuckoo likes,
And so do I;
When showers betumble the chestnut spikes,
And nestlings fly;
And the little brown nightingale bills his best,
And they sit outside at "The Travellers Rest",
And maids come forth sprig-muslin drest,
And citizens dream of the south and west,
And so do I.

Thomas Hardy,
English novelist and poet,
1840–1928
From "Weathers"

112

A thing of beauty is a joy forever:
Its loveliness increases; it will never
Pass into nothingness; but still will keep
A bower quiet for us, and a sleep
Full of sweet dreams, and health, and
   quiet breathing.

John Keats,
English Romantic poet,
1795–1821
From "Endymion"

113

Non omnis moriar.
I shall not altogether die.

Horace,
Roman lyric poet,
65 BCE–8 BCE

114

But suddenly, we know not how, a sound
Of living streams, an odour, a flower crowned
With dew, a lark up springing from the sod,
And we awake. O joy and deep amaze!
Beneath the everlasting hills we stand,
We hear the voices of the morning seas,
And earnest prophesyings in the land,
While from the open heaven leans forth at gaze
The encompassing great cloud of witnesses.

Edward Dowden,
Irish poet,
1843–1913
From "Awakening"

115

There are only two days in the year that nothing can be done. One is called Yesterday, and the other is called Tomorrow. Today is the right day to Love, Believe, Do and mostly Live.

Anonymous

116

The Owl and the Pussy-Cat went to sea
In a beautiful pea-green boat:
They took some honey, and plenty of
  money,
Wrapped up in a five-pound note.
The Owl looked up to the stars above,
And sang to a small guitar,
"O lovely Pussy! O Pussy, my love,
What a beautiful Pussy you are,
You are,
You are!
What a beautiful Pussy you are!"

Edward Lear,
English artist and poet,
1812–1888
From "The Owl and the Pussy-Cat"

117

If you press me to say why I loved him, I can say no more then it was because he was he and I was I.

Michel de Montaigne,
French Renaissance philosopher and essayist,
1533–1592
(of his friend Étienne de la Boétie)

118

Through simplicity comes great beauty.

Anonymous

119

I can never feel certain of its truth but from a clear perception of its beauty.

John Keats,
English Romantic poet,
1795–1821
From a letter dated 16 December 1819

120

Let the beauty of what you love be what you do.

Rumi,
Persian poet and mystic,
1207–1273

121

To be beautiful means to be yourself. You don't need to be accepted by others. All you need is to accept yourself.

Anonymous

123

The soul that sees beauty may sometimes walk alone.

Johann Wolfgang von Goethe,
German writer, philosopher and poet,
1749–1832

124

There is nothing that makes its way more directly to the soul then beauty.

Joseph Addison,
English writer, poet and politician,
1672–1719

125

The only lasting beauty is the beauty of the heart.

Rumi,
Persian poet and mystic,
1207–1273

126

Beauty is being the best version of yourself inside and out.

Anonymous

127

Do not desire her beauty in your heart, nor let it capture you with her eyelids.

Old Testament, Proverbs 6:25

128

Love of beauty is taste.
The creation of beauty is art.

Ralph Waldo Emerson,
American essayist and poet,
1803–1882

129

Your beauty should not come from outward adornment, such as elaborate hairstyles and the wearing of gold jewellery or fine clothes. Rather, it should be that of your inner self, the unfading beauty of a gentle and quiet spirit, which is of great worth in God's sight.

New Testament, 1 Peter 3:3–4

130

It's amazing how complete is the delusion that beauty is goodness.

Leo Tolstoy,
Russian author,
1828–1910
From *The Kreutzer Sonata*

131

The power of finding beauty
in the humblest of things
makes home happy and
life lovely.

Louise May Alcott,
American novelist and poet,
1832–1888

132

Give everyday the chance to become the most beautiful day of your life.

Mark Twain,
American writer and novelist,
1835–1910

133

Beauty's voice speaks gently: it creeps only into the most awakened souls.

Friedrich Nietzsche,
German philosopher,
1844–1900

134

Dwell on the beauty of life. Watch the stars, and see yourself running with them.

Marcus Aurelius,
Roman emperor and Stoic philosopher,
121–180 CE

135

Little brown brother, oh! little brown
  brother,
Are you awake in the dark?
Here we lie cosily, close to each other;
Hark to the song of the lark –
"Waken!" the lark says, "waken and dress
  you;
Put on your green coats and gay,
Blue sky will shine on you, sunshine
  caress you –
Waken! 'tis morning – 'tis May!"

Edith Bland,
English author and poet,
1858–1924
From "Baby Seed Song"

136

Beauty is an attitude.

Anonymous

137

You are so hard on yourself.
Take a moment.
Sit back.
Marvel at your life:
   At the grief that softened you
   At the heartache that wisened you,
   At the suffering that strengthened
      you.
Despite everything,
You still grow.
Be proud
Of this.

Anonymous

138

You are altogether beautiful, my darling, and there is no blemish in you.

Old Testament, Song of Solomon 4:7

139

She is not fair to outward view
As many maidens be;
Her loveliness I never knew
Until she smiled on me.

Hartley Coleridge,
English poet, biographer, essayist, and teacher,
1796–1849
From "She Is Not Fair"

140

The earth laughs in flowers.

Ralph Waldo Emerson,
American essayist and poet,
1803–1882

GROWTH
SUMMER

We have been taught to believe that there is a whole side of life that relies on cause and effect. Shakespeare said, "Every why hath a wherefore." If there were no causes there would be no effects, and if nothing came from nothing, we would not exist. Therefore, the axis for our being is determined by a "something" which leads to something else. Chance and change fuse together to produce a new entity. As day follows night, the world spins, the quiet of winter prepares the earth for the spring. Leaves patch into the sky, blossom floats like confetti on a lazy breeze, and seeds develop into new crops. A whole world is born again out of the past, and as it grows into fruition, it is sowing the future.

None of this could happen if the conditions for growth, and the processes of reproduction, were inhospitable. The natural circumstances that come together, the chances taken, the curious coincidences, the baffling acts of fate, all become a part of life's great adventure as we move on. We are constantly nurtured by the world around us while we grow within that world. We are an intrinsic part of everything that goes on around us.

QUESTIONS TO REFLECT ON

Here the questions to ask yourself take the form of a short reflection about growth.

❖ Imagine that I am holding out a blank sheet of paper for you to look at. Then imagine that the paper is speaking to you very quietly. It is asking you questions, and it smiles gently at you as it says . . .

Can you see the sun in me,
Can you feel the wind?
Can you hear the rain pitter-patter?
Can you see the seed growing,
Can you touch the leaves unfurling,
Can you find the tree in me?
Can you hear the bumblebee humming,
Can you smell the rain coming,
The river swelling?
Can you hear the children playing,
Can you hear the loggers saw,
Can you catch the tree falling,
Can you watch, as it sails away
Can you hear the mill wheels turning?
Can you sense my paper me?
Can you see the sun drying,
Can you feel me changing?
Can you take me, write me,
Can you find the words?
Can you sign your name,
Can you, can you . . . thank me?

A poem could be all of these questions lying hidden in
a piece of paper, or printed over the page in a book. It is
the result of ideas and notions coming together in forms
of rhythm and rhyme, in stanzas, in haiku and sonnets, in
the many, many different ways of writing. Sometimes its
meaning is hidden, and you have to read between the lines;
sometimes it unlocks a rich stream of thoughts that distract
you from your problems. Ultimately it is the effect of millions
of causes, of many productions, and changes, and growth,
until it rests kindly in front of you one day in the form of a
poem or a saying, or a quote.

   Can you feel how supported by and interconnected you
are to everything around you?

141

What greater thing is there for two human souls, than to feel that they are joined for life – strengthen each other ... to be one with each other in silent unspeakable memories

George Eliot, pen name of Mary Ann Evans,
English novelist, poet, journalist and translator,
1819–1880
From *Adam Bede*

122

Beauty is not in the face;
beauty is a light in the heart.

Khalil Gibran,
Lebanese-American writer and poet,
1883–1931

142

Eternity is in love with the
productions of time.

William Blake,
English poet, painter and printmaker,
1757–1827

143

The thistledown's flying, though the winds are all still,
On the green grass now lying, now mounting the hill,
The spring from the fountain now boils like a pot;
Through stones past the counting it bubbles red-hot.

The ground parched and cracked is like overbaked
   bread,
The greensward all wracked is, bents dried up and
   dead.
The fallow fields glitter like water indeed,
And gossamers twitter, flung from weed unto weed.

Hill-tops like hot iron glitter bright in the sun,
And the rivers we're eying burn to gold as they run;
Burning hot is the ground, liquid gold is the air;
Whoever looks round sees Eternity there.

John Clare,
English poet,
1793–1864
"Autumn"

144

If God did not exist, it would be necessary to invent him.

Voltaire,
French Enlightenment writer,
1694–1778

145

Where the thistle lifts a purple crown
Six foot out of the turf,
And the harebell shakes on windy hill –
O breath of the distant surf! –

The hills look over on the South,
And southward dreams the sea;
And with the sea-breeze hand in hand
Came innocence and she.

Where 'mid the gorse the raseberry
Red for the gatherer springs,
Two children did we stray and talk
Wise, idle, childish things.

Oh, there were flowers in Storrington
On the turf and on the spray:
But the sweetest flower on Sussex hills
Was the Daisy-flower that day!

Francis Thompson,
English poet,
1859–1907
From "Daisy"

146

Materiam superabat opus.
The workmanship surpassed
the material.

Ovid,
Roman poet,
43 BCE–17 CE

147

Yes. I remember Adlestrop –
The name, because one afternoon
Of heat the express-train drew up there
Unwontedly. It was late June.

The stream hissed. Some one cleared his throat.
No one left and no one came
On the bare platform. What I saw
Was Adelstrop – only the name

And willows, willow-herb, and grass,
The meadowsweet, the haystacks dry,
No whit less still the lonely fair
Than the high cloudlets in the sky.

And for that minute a blackbird sang
Close by, and round him mistier,
Farther and farther, all the birds
Of Oxfordshire and Gloucestershire.

Edward Thomas,
English poet, essayist and novelist,
1878–1917
"Adelstrop"

148

How many seconds in a minute?
Sixty, and no more in it.

How many minutes in an hour?
Sixty for sun and shower.

How many hours in a day?
Twenty-four both to work and play.

How many days in a week?
Seven both to hear and speak.

How many weeks in a month?
Four, as the swift moon runneth.

How many months in a year?
Twelve the almanac makes clear.

How many years in an age?
One hundred says the sage.

How many ages in time?
No one knows the rhyme.

Christina Rossetti,
English poet,
1830–1894
"How Many Seconds in a Minute?"

149

Veil after veil of thin dusky gauze is lifted, and by degrees the forms and colours of things are restored to them, and we watch the dawn remaking the world in its antique pattern.

Oscar Wilde,
Irish novelist and playwright,
1854–1900
From *The Picture of Dorian Gray*

150

Three hundred years growing
The hundred years living
Three hundred years dying.

The life of an oak, according to an old saying

151

Be not afraid of growing
slowly, be afraid only of
standing still.

Chinese Proverb

152

Golden slumbers kiss your eyes,
Smiles awake you when you rise,
Sleep pretty wantons, do not cry,
And I will sing a lullabye,
Rock them, rock them lullabye.

Thomas Dekker,
English dramatist and writer,
1570–1641
From "Golden Slumbers"

153

Childhood is that wonderful time of life when all you need to do to lose weight is take a bath.

Anonymous

154

A man who gives his children habits of industry provides for them a better fortune than by giving them fortune.

Richard Whately,
English theologian,
1787–1863

155

When you need to get something done, ask a busy woman.

Anonymous

156

No time like the present.

Delarivier Manley,
English author and playwright,
1696–1724
From *The Lost Lover*

157

Three centuries he grows, and
   three he stays
Supreme in state, and in three
   more decays.

John Dryden,
English literary critic, translator,
playwright and first Poet Laureate,
1631–1700

158

You are no ruin, sir – no lightning struck tree: you are green and vigorous. Plants will grow about your roots, whether you ask them or not.

Charlotte Brontë,
English novelist and poet,
1816–1855
Jane Eyre to Mr Rochester after he had
lost his sight in the fire, from *Jane Eyre*

159

Therefore, with resolution as his only support and companion, he set his mind on enlightenment and proceeded to the root of a Bo-Tree, where the ground was carpeted with green grass.

From "Life of Buddha"
trans. Tenzin Chōgyel (1701–1767), Bhutan

160

Thou wert a bauble once, a cup and
  ball
Which babes might play with;
And the thievish jay,
Seeking her food, with ease might have
  purloined, the auburn nut …

William Cowper,
English poet,
1731–1800
From "The Yardly Oak"

161

How doth the little busy bee,
Improve each shining hour,
And gather honey all the day
From every opening flower.

Issac Watts,
English minister, hymn-writer,
theologian, and logician,
1674–1748
From "How Doth the Little Busy Bee"

162

Adam and Eve had many advantages, but the principal one was that they escaped teething.

Mark Twain,
American writer and novelist,
1835–1910

163

Mistress Mary, Quite contrary,
How does your garden grow?
With Silver Bells and Cockle
  Shells,
And pretty maids all in a row.

17th-century nursery rhyme, generally
thought to refer to Mary Queen of Scots,
the growth of her reign, the Roman Catholic
Church, and her unfaithful husband.

164

Oh, what a power is motherhood, possessing a potent spell. All women alike fight fiercely for a child.

Euripides,
Greek dramatist and philosopher,
480–406 BCE

165

Have big dreams. You'll grow into them.

Anonymous

166

Mighty oaks from little acorns grow.

English proverb

167

These successes encourage: they can because they think they can.

Virgil,
Roman poet,
70 BCE–19 BCE

168

It is not because things are difficult that we do not dare; it is because we do not dare that they're difficult.

Seneca,
Roman Stoic philosopher,
4 BCE–65 CE

169

As we advance in life it becomes more and more difficult, but in fighting the difficulties the inmost strength of the heart is developed.

Vincent Van Gogh,
Dutch post-impressionist painter,
1853–1890
From *Letters to Theo*

170

Everyone should carefully observe which way his heart draws him, and then choose that way with all his strength.

Hasidic saying

171

You have power over your mind – not outside events. Realize this, and you will find strength.

Marcus Aurelius,
Roman emperor and Stoic philosopher,
121–180 CE

172

Physical strength is measured by what we carry.
Inner strength is measured by what we can bear.

Anonymous

173

Spirit has fifty times the strength and staying power of brawn and muscle.

Mark Twain,
American writer and novelist,
1835–1910

174

He who conquers others is strong; he who conquers himself is mighty.

Lao Tzu,
Chinese philosopher and writer,
6th/4th century BCE

175

What we achieve inwardly will change outer reality.

Plutarch,
Roman essayist and biographer,
64–120 CE

176

I think she is growing up, and so begins to dream dreams, and have hopes and fears and fidgets, without knowing why or being able to explain them.

Louise May Alcott,
American novelist and poet,
1832–1888
From *Little Women*

177

Cowards die many times
before their deaths, the valiant
never taste of death but once.

William Shakespeare,
English playwright,
1564–1616
From *Julius Caesar*, Act II Scene 2

178

Twenty years from now you will be more disappointed by the things that you didn't do then by the ones you did do. So throw off the bowlines. Sail away from the safe harbour. Catch the trade winds in your sails. Explore. Dream. Discover.

Mark Twain,
American writer and novelist,
1835–1910

PROSPERITY
SUMMER–AUTUMN

This section of the book is focused on the idea of prosperity and its attendant themes of abundance, wealth and expansion. Our quest is to look at the value of the most simple and sometimes under-appreciated things in life, the small and the beautiful, the invaluable observations that money can't buy.

It is very normal in our society to follow the general hedonistic inclination to achieve more; to want to earn vast amounts of money; to seek pleasure from spending it and to expand the world we live in with the addition of luxury items, buying presents and enhancing our material world with all the acquisitions that we can accumulate for the extension of our personal happiness.

Life, however, is not always quite so simple and there will be times when – no matter how rich you are, nor how content you have felt with your existence – a moment will occur when you may need protection from illness, ageing or loss of life. There is a counterbalance to those privileged moments of comfort when suddenly anxiety and distress can creep in and darken the world around us.

In those times you need to see that prosperity is not just about what we own or the things we long to acquire; it is a way of thinking. It is a mindset. It is not about how much money we might have, it is about how rich we can be without very much at all. It is about appreciating time, and how we can use it best; it is about finding a more meaningful and lasting way to spend this precious time. Henry David Thoreau, a 19th-century American philosopher once said, "I am happy with what I am and what I have . . . for my wealth is not a possession but enjoyment."

Reflect on the aspects of life which help us find a moment's peace, a moment to enjoy what we have already, the moment when we can release our grip on negative thoughts, and relax the hold we have on the things we feel so attached to.

You can begin a day positively by concentrating on achieving one "good" thing. You can open a book and let yourself unwind in the safety of other people's words. You can feel the wisdom within the sayings. You can share this with others. There is a belief that if you make someone smile in the morning and help someone who is sad in the afternoon, then you will achieve inner prosperity. You can transfer the power of wisdom and kindness and expand your horizons, as you lighten the load for those worse off than yourself. This is enrichment beyond self. There may be a great deal of truth in the wisdom of counting your blessings. These are some of the most invaluable lessons to learn and to appreciate, from taking some time to read a poem to sharing a few well-said words.

Poets and philosophers have devoted much time in the past to reflecting on what it truly means to be prosperous, or what sacrifices are made in the name of becoming richer, and of how it might feel to lose it all. This is something that can worry everyone. Poems and quotations have the power to enhance our understanding by opening up other perspectives or by explaining and reaffirming what we already know. They have a way of uncovering the notion that we may be far richer than we think. They can gently remind us that we are not alone and they may go so far as to persuade us to set aside the past and not get lost in the future. They can evoke memories and revive hope; they can help with the making of plans, and they can untangle confusion.

QUESTIONS TO REFLECT ON

❖ What do you think about money? About wealth?

❖ Are you richer than you think?

❖ How deserving do you believe yourself to be?

❖ Could you find contentment in the natural world around you, if all else fails?

Perhaps the most important question to ask when meditating on the themes of prosperity and abundance, is this: How can I honour and spend my real riches, the time that I have with those closest to me?

179

Three best to have in plenty –
sunshine, wisdom, and
generousity.

Irish Triad

180

My heart is like a singing bird,
Whose nest is in a watered shoot;
My heart is like an apple tree
Whose boughs are bent with thickset fruit.
My heart is like a rainbow shell
That paddles in a halcyon sea;
My heart is gladder than all these
Because my love is come to me.

Raise me a dais of silk and down,
Hang it with vair and purple dyes;
Carve it in doves, and pomegranates,
And peacocks with a hundred eyes;
Work it in gold and silver grapes,
In leaves, and silver fleurs-de-lys;
Because the birthday of my life
Is come, my love is come to me.

Christina Rossetti,
English poet,
1830–1894
From "A Birthday"

181

The highest service demands the greatest sacrifice, but it secures the fullest blessing and the greatest fruitfulness.

James Hudson Taylor,
British missionary in China,
1832–1905

182

Season of mists and mellow fruitfulness,
Close bosom-friend of the maturing sun;
Conspiring with him how to load and bless
With fruit the vines that round the thatch-eves
    run;
To bend with apples and mossed cottage trees,
And fill all fruit with ripeness to the core;
To swell the gourd, and plump the hazel shells
With a sweet kernel; to set budding more,
And still more, later flowers for the bees,
Until they think warm days will never cease,
For Summer has o'er-brimm'd their clammy cells.

John Keats,
English Romantic poet,
1795–1821
From "To Autumn"

183

Those who know when they have enough are rich.

Chinese proverb

184

No matter how much faculty of idle seeing a man has, the step from knowing to doing is rarely taken, it is a step out of a chalk circle of imbecility into fruitfulness.

Ralph Waldo Emerson,
American essayist and poet,
1803–1882

185

The fruit of the Spirit is Love, Joy, Peace, Forbearance, Kindness, Goodness and Faithfulness.

New Testament, Epistle to the Galatians 5:22

186

The secret of reaping the greatest fruitfulness and greatest enjoyment from life is to live dangerously.

Friedrich Nietzsche,
German philosopher,
1844–1900

187

A blessing is fruitful and always prosperous.

Old Testament, Psalm 1:3

188

Over the land is April,
Over my heart a rose,
Over the high, brown mountain
The sound of singing goes.
Say, love, do you hear me
Hear my sonnets ring,
Over the high, brown mountain,
Love, do you hear me sing.

By highway, love, and byway
The snows succeed the rose,
Over the high, brown mountain
The wind of winter blows.
Say, love, do you hear me,
Hear my sonnets ring?
Over the high, brown mountain
I sound the song of spring,
I throw the flowers of spring.
Do you hear the song of spring?
Hear you the songs of spring?

Robert Lewis Stevenson,
Scottish novelist, poet and travel writer,
1850–1894
"Over the Land is April"

189

Great wealth is a gift from heaven; moderate wealth results from frugality.

Chinese proverb

190

Satan threatens you with poverty
And enjoins you to be niggardly
Whereas Allah promises you
  forgiveness and prosper
And Allah is Ample-Giving
And He knows everything ...

Quran, 2. 268

191

Forever is composed of nows.

Emily Dickinson,
American poet,
1830–1886

192

At once I'm in a boat
but sailing sunward …

(Hard is the journey,
Hard is the journey,
So many turnings,
And now where am I?)

So when the breeze breaks waves,
bringing fair weather,
I set a cloud for sails,
cross the blue oceans!

Li Po,
Chinese poet,
701–762
From "Hard is the Journey"
Trans. L. Cramer-Byng, 1909

193

Sumer is Icumen in,
Loudly sing, cuckoo!
Grows the seed and blows the mead,
And springs the wood anew;
Sing cuckoo!
Ewe bleats harshly after lamb,
Cows and calves make moo;
Bullock stamps and deer champs,
Now shrilly sing, cuckoo!
Cuckoo! Cuckoo!
Wild bird are you;
Be never still, cuckoo!

Anonymous medieval English round song

194

Who has children cannot long remain poor; who has none cannot remain rich.

Chinese Proverb

195

I am wealthy in more ways than one.
I am wealthy in more ways than one.
I am wealthy in more ways than one.

Anonymous

196

First cherry
budding
by peach blossoms.

Matsuo Bashō,
Japanese poet,
1644–1694

197

Fogur gaithe
Fri fid flescach
Forglas neol;
Essa aba,
Esnad ala,
Alainn ceol

Sound of the wind in a branching wood,
Grey cloud;
River-falls,
Cry of a swan –
Beautiful music.

Anonymous Gaelic poem

198

Through the closed blinds the
   golden sun
Poured in a dusty beam,
Like the celestial ladder seen
By Jacob in his dream.

Henry Wadsworth Longfellow,
American poet and educator,
1807–1882
From "A Gleam of Sunshine"

199

The blackbird sings a loud strain,
To him the live wood is a heritage,
The sad angry sea is fallen asleep,
The speckled salmon leaps.
The sun smiles over every land,
A parting for me from the brood of cares:
Hounds bark, stags tryst, ravens flourish,
Summer is come!

Anonymous
From "Summer Has Come",
10th-century Irish poem

200

That it will never come again is what
  makes life so sweet.
Dwell in possibility.
Find ecstasy in life;
The mere sense of living is joy enough.

Emily Dickinson,
American poet,
1830–1886

201

'Tis better to spend money like there's no tomorrow then to spend tonight like there's no money!

Anonymous

202

A wet and windy May fills the barn with corn and hay.

Irish saying

203

If you are planning for a year, sow rice, if you are planning for a decade, plant trees, if you are planning for a lifetime, educate people.

Chinese proverb

204

Yellow rose petals
thunder –
a waterfall.

Matsuo Bashō,
Japanese poet,
1644–1694

205

I am rich beyond the dreams of avarice.

Edward Moore,
English dramatist,
1712–1757
From *The Gamester*

206

If thou art rich, thou'rt poor;
For, like an ass whose back with ingots
   bows,
Thou bear'st thy heavy riches but a
   journey,
And death unloads thee.

William Shakespeare,
English playwright,
1564–1616
From *Measure for Measure*, Act III Scene 1

207

You are richer then you think.

Anonymous

208

Do all the good you can,
By all the means that you can,
In all the ways that you can,
To all the people that you can,
As long as ever you can.

John Wesley,
English cleric,
1703–1791
"Money Does Not Buy Happiness"

209

Good words are worth much,
and cost little.

George Herbert,
Welsh poet,
1593–1632

210

It is better to return a borrowed pot with a little something you last cooked in it.

Native American proverb

No act of kindness no matter how small is ever wasted.

Aesop,
Greek fabulist and storyteller,
c.620–564 BCE

212

The deep Stillness
Seeping into the rocks
The voice of Cicadas.

Matsuo Bashō,
Japanese poet,
1644–1694

213

Without kindness there can be no true joy.

Thomas Carlyle,
Scottish historian and essayist,
1795–1881

214

May I reach
That purest heaven, be to other souls
The cup of strength in some great agony,
Enkindle generous ardour, feed pure love,
Beget the smiles that have no cruelty,
Be the sweet presence of a good diffused,
And in diffusion ever more intense!
So shall I join the choir invisible
Whose music is the gladness of the world.

George Eliot, pen name of Mary Ann Evans,
English novelist, poet, journalist and translator,
1819–1880
From "The Choir Invisible"

215

There is a sort of gratification in doing good which makes us rejoice in ourselves.

Michel de Montaigne,
French Renaissance philosopher and essayist,
1533–1592

216

The true harvest of my life
Is intangible
A little star dust caught,
A portion of the rainbow
I have clutched.

Henry David Thoreau,
American philosopher, essayist and poet,
1817–1862

217

No race can prosper till it learns there is as much dignity in tilling a field as in writing a poem.

Booker T. Washington,
American educator and author,
1856–1915

218

I know a bank where the wild thyme blows,
Where oxlips and the nodding violet grows,
Quite over-canopied with luscious woodbine,
With sweet musk-roses and with eglantine
There sleeps Titania sometime of the night,
Lulled in these flowers with dances and delight.

William Shakespeare,
English playwright,
1564–1616
From *A Midsummer Night's Dream*, Act II Scene 1

219

Midsummer night is not long but it sets many cradles rocking.

Swedish proverb

220

Sweet moon, I thank thee for thy sunny
   beams;
I thank thee, Moon, for shining now so
   bright.

William Shakespeare,
English playwright,
1564–1616
From *A Midsummer Night's Dream*, Act V Scene 1

221

I will give you thanks with my whole heart.

Old Testament, Psalms 138:1

222

Creator, open our hearts to peace and
healing between all people.
Creator, open our hearts, to provide and
protect for all children of the earth.
Creator, open our hearts.

Native American Mi' Kmaq prayer at Thanksgiving

Hand in hand, with this faery grace,
Will we sing, and bless this place.

William Shakespeare,
English playwright,
1564–1616
From *A Midsummer Night's Dream*, Act V Scene 2

HARMONY
AUTUMN

Harmony, balance and prudence (such a lovely old-fashioned word meaning "caution") are what define nature at its best. These three "graces" are something we aspire to, but often they don't come easily to us in everyday life. Caution and balance create and protect harmony, and when either of them is forgotten, the harmony that has existed is undermined.

There is an old Buddhist story about the restoration of harmony after a stark division took place within a group of monks. Ultimately it threatened to break up the monastery. A small domestic oversight had suddenly escalated when blame was levelled at the monk who had forgotten to wash his own bowl. Prudence was lost as tempers flared and the balance within the community disintegrated. Everyone started to take sides and argue. Eventually the Buddha was called upon, and when he saw that the precious harmony within the community was endangered, he wrote down some special guidelines which would help to maintain the concord among groups of people and families in the future. He noted that in order to share equally, and in a balanced way, we have to watch our individualism and not let it overwhelm others; we must be mindful of the words we choose, as often they can be misconstrued and cause harm; we must truly listen to both sides of an argument; and lastly, we must be constantly aware of how often we jump to conclusions and cast judgement. The better conclusions are taken by sharing responsibility, with everyone in agreement. In other words, harmony in a community needs to be cared for in much the same way that you might care for a loved one.

In the natural world, there are conditions which guide the development of all living matter and which provide the circumstances for expansion and growth. These prosper when there is a harmony between the elements.

Nothing can exist on its own. A heart can't beat without blood circulating through its ventricles; a brain can't function without oxygen; a smile won't happen without twenty-six muscles flexing all together at the same time, and knowledge cannot be acquired without experience and an inquisitive mind.

Harmony can be compared to a kaleidoscope. The tiny pieces of coloured glass shift into a symmetry every time they are moved to create a new pattern. Every pattern is different, but equally every pattern is balanced. In life harmonies take on many forms, in many different ways, providing a cohesive strength at the core of our existence, because without it we would suffer from immeasurable chaos. Our lives are balanced by harmonies which can include everything, from quantum physics to the shapes of snowflakes, to complimentary colours, to combinations of delicious tastes – and all these aspects must, in turn, be supported with caution and perspicacity.

In general, people love music because of a particular arrangement of beats, sequences of sounds and vibrations that please and inspire the senses. Three notes – for example, C, G and upper C – combine to create a chord. When we mix colours the three primaries, red, yellow and blue, can produce a myriad of others. A ceramic pot cannot be made without clay, air and water. The success of any of these processes relies (to a degree) on harmony and balance.

Nature is clearly defined by harmony and balance, but as humans we have to create our own balance if we are going to establish a solid understanding of ourselves and the world around us. Nature's harmonies seem to happen spontaneously, whereas we humans have to "intend" to create a sound, a colour or an object. We employ intellectual checks and balances to achieve these solutions. We also, naturally, rely on the harmonies of others and the world around us in the balancing act of creating peace. In order to do this we must be consciously aware that our own equilibrium is based most often on inner and outer harmony.

Without doubt, words have played a significant part in contributing to our understanding of harmony and balance. Their sounds can be measured out in beat, rhyme, phrase, alliteration and cadence. Words share knowledge and feeling; they have a harmony not only with each other but with a higher state of being, or wisdom. They are threaded onto a cloth of many colours, quilted and patched up over time. Words can also stand the test of time, can last longer than our own existence and can continue to shine a magical light into our daily lives and onto the lives of those to come.

By seeking out the poems and sayings in this collection, and reflecting on their meanings, we orchestrate our emotions and intellect to find another source of inner harmony and support for our own private lives once again.

QUESTIONS TO REFLECT ON

❖ Are you seeking harmony within yourself, or creating harmony externally?

❖ Are harmony and balance connected to beauty?

❖ Are inner and outer wellbeing dependent on the harmonies within and without ourselves?

❖ Can you balance what you need in life with what you want out of life?

Inner harmony and balance are known to flourish when you cautiously detach your memory from pursuing the past, and your mind from getting lost in the future. The reading of a poem or a few wise words helps to hold you still or helps you pause for just a moment to reflect on the "invisible" present.

224

In the twilight rain
these brilliant-hued hibiscus –
A lovely sunset.

Matsuo Bashō,
Japanese poet,
1644–1694

225

Prosperity is no just scale; adversity is the only balance to weigh friends.

Plutarch,
Roman essayist and biographer,
64–120 CE

226

Knowing is not enough; we must apply.
Willing is not enough; we must do.

Johann Wolfgang von Goethe,
German writer, philosopher and poet,
1749–1832

227

The best and safest thing is to keep a balance in your life, acknowledge the great powers around us and in us.
If you can do that, and live that way, you are really a wise man.

Euripides,
Greek dramatist and philosopher,
480–406 BCE

228

For as the Moon is thus led by its angel, the Heavens draw near to Balance.

Nostradamus,
French astrologer, physician and seer,
1503–1566

229

The life that I have chosen gives me my full hours of enjoyment for the balance of my life: the sun will not rise, or set, without my notice and thanks.

Winslow Homer,
American painter and printmaker,
1836–1910

230

Fall, leaves, fall; die, flowers, away;
Lengthen night and shorten day;
Every leaf speaks bliss to me
Fluttering from the autumn tree.
I shall smile when wreaths of snow
Blossom where the rose should grow;
I shall sing when night's decay
Ushers in a drearier day.

Emily Brontë,
English novelist and poet,
1818–1848
"Fall, Leaves, Fall"

231

As soon as you can trust yourself, you will know how to live.

Johann Wolfgang von Goethe,
German writer, philosopher and poet,
1749–1832

232

To see a World in a Grain of Sand,
And a Heaven in a Wild Flower,
Hold Infinity in the palm of your hand
And Eternity in an hour.

William Blake,
English poet, painter and printmaker,
1757–1827
From "Auguries of Innocence"

233

Soul meets soul on lovers' lips.

Percy Bysshe Shelley,
English Romantic poet,
1792–1822

234

In nature we never see anything isolated, but everything in connection with something else which is before it, beside it, under it, and over it.

Johann Wolfgang von Goethe,
German writer, philosopher and poet,
1749–1832

235

If you add a little to a little,
And then do it again,
Soon that little shall be much.

Hesoid,
Greek poet,
c.750–c.650 BCE

236

When we create peace, harmony and balance in our minds we will find it in our lives.

Anonymous

237

To put everything in balance is good, to put everything in harmony is better.

Victor Hugo,
French writer,
1802–1885

238

Carelessness in dressing is moral suicide.

Honoré de Balzac,
French novelist and playwright,
1799–1850

239

He who lives in harmony with himself lives in harmony with the world.

Marcus Aurelius,
Roman emperor and Stoic philosopher,
121–180 CE

240

Carefulness costs you nothing.
Carelessness may cost you
   your life.

Anonymous

241

Lead, Kindly Light, amidst th'encircling
 gloom,
Lead Thou me on!
The night is dark, and I am far from
 home –
Lead thou me on!
Keep Thou my feet; I do not ask to see
The distant scene; one step enough
 for me.

John Henry Newman,
English theologian and poet,
1801–1890
From "Lead, Kindly Light" (hymn)

242

The most happy man is he who knows how to bring into relation the end and beginning of his life.

Johann Wolfgang von Goethe,
German writer, philosopher and poet,
1749–1832

243

The man who moves a mountain begins by carrying away small stones.

Confucius,
Chinese philosopher,
551–479 BCE

244

The best way to cheer yourself up is to try to cheer somebody else up.

Mark Twain,
American writer and novelist,
1835–1910

245

Be careless in your dress if you must, but keep a tidy soul.

Mark Twain,
American writer and novelist,
1835–1910

246

The journey of a thousand miles begins with one step.

Lao Tzu,
Chinese philosopher and writer,
6th/4th century BCE

247

How sweet the moonlight sleeps upon the bank!
Here we will sit, and let the sounds of music
Creep in our ears: soft stillness and the night
Become touches of sweet harmony.
Sit, Jessica: look, how the floor of heaven
Is thick with patines of bright gold:
There's not the smallest orb which thou behold'sy
But in his motion like an angel sings,
Still quiring to the young-eyed cherubins;
Such harmony is in immortal souls;
But, whilst this muddy vesture of decay
Doth grossly close it in, we cannot hear it.

William Shakespeare,
English playwright,
1564–1616
From *The Merchant of Venice*, Act V Scene 1

248

Such sweet compulsion doth in music lie.

John Milton,
English poet,
1608–1674
From *Arcades*

249

Ring out ye crystal spheres,
Once bless our human ears
(if ye have powers to touch our
   senses so)
And let your silver chime
Move in melodious time;
And let the base of heav'ns deep
   organ blow,
And with ninefold harmony
Make up full consort to th'angelic
   symphony.

John Milton,
English poet,
1608–1674

250

While with an eye made quiet by the
   power
Of harmony, and the deep power of joy,
We see into the life of things.

William Wordsworth,
English Romantic poet,
1770–1850

251

From harmony, from heavenly harmony
This universal frame began:
From harmony to harmony
Through all the compass of the notes
  it ran,
The diapason closing full in Man.

John Dryden,
English literary critic, translator,
playwright and first Poet Laureate,
1631–1700
From "A Song for St Cecilia's Day"

252

Teach me half the gladness
That thy brain must know,
Such harmonious madness
From my lips would flow
The world should listen then – as I am
  listening now.

Percy Bysshe Shelley,
English Romantic poet,
1792–1822
From "To a Skylark"

253

To many, total abstinence
is easier then perfect
moderation.

Saint Augustine,
Roman African theologian and philosopher,
354–430 CE

254

Every human benefit, every virtue and every prudent act, is founded on compromise.

Edmund Burke,
Irish statesman and philosopher,
1729–1797
From "On Conciliation with America"

255

Whatever you do, do cautiously, and look to the end.

Anonymous Latin anecdote from *Gesta Romanorum*

Blessed are the poor in spirit: for theirs is the
kingdom of heaven.

Blessed are they that mourn: for they shall be
comforted.

Blessed are the meek: for they shall inherit the
earth.

Blessed are they which hunger and thirst after
righteousness: for they shall be filled.

Blessed are the merciful: for they shall obtain
mercy.

Blessed are the poor of heart: for they shall see
God.

Blessed are the peacemakers: for they shall be
called the Children of God.

New Testament, Matthew 5:3

257

Invisible harmony is better than visible.

Heraclius,
Roman emperor of the Byzantine Empire,
c.575–641 CE

258

Stone walls do not a prison make
Nor iron bars a cage;
Minds innocent and quiet take
That for a hermitage;
If I have freedom in my love,
And in my soul am free;
Angels alone, that soar above,
Enjoy such liberty.

Richard Lovelace,
English poet,
1618–1658
From "To Althea, From Prison"

259

How tuneful is the voice of the sea,
What true accord in ocean's murmur,
And in the reeds light, rhythmic tremor
What tender musicality!

In nature all is harmony,
A consonance fore'er agreed on,
And 'tis alone our phantom freedom
That is disturbing off-key.

Fyodor Ivanovich Tyutchev,
Russian poet,
1803–1873
From "How Tuneful is the Voice of the Sea"
trans. Vladimir Nobokov

260

Often rebuked, yet always back returning
To those first feelings that were born in me,
And leaving busy chase of wealth and learning
For idle dreams of things which cannot be:

Today, I will not seek the shadowy region;
Its unsustaining vastness waxes drear;
And visions rising, legion after legion,
Bring the unreal world too strangely near.

I'll walk, but not in old heroic traces,
And not in paths of high morality,
And not amongst the half-distinguished faces,
The clouded forms of long-past history.

I'll walk where my own nature would be
    leading:
It vexes me to choose another guide:
Where grey flocks in ferny glens are feeding;
Where the wild wind blows on the mountain
    side.

What have these lonely mountains worth
    revealing?
More glory and more grief than I can tell:
The earth that wakes one human heart to
    feeling
Can centre both the worlds of Heaven and
    Hell.

Emily Brontë,
English novelist and poet,
1818–1848

261

While with an eye made quiet by the
  power
Of harmony, and the deep power of joy,
We see into the life of things.

William Wordsworth,
English Romantic poet,
1770–1850
From "Lines Composed a Few Miles Above
Tintern Abbey, On Revisiting the Banks
of the Wye During a Tour. July 13, 1798"

262

Every thought that we put into the world affects it. Think love, think peace, think harmony.

Anonymous

263

It is not in the stars to hold our destiny but in ourselves.

William Shakespeare,
English playwright,
1564–1616

264

Observe good faith and justice toward all nations.
Cultivate peace and harmony with all.

George Washington,
American president of the
United States of America,
1732–1799

265

The hidden harmony is better then the obvious.

Alexander Pope,
English poet,
1688–1744

266

Harmony is called the eternal. Knowing the eternal is called clarity.

Lao Tzu,
Chinese philosopher and writer,
6th/4th century BCE

267

Art is a harmony parallel with nature.

Paul Cézanne,
French post-impressionist painter,
1839–1906

268

Beauty of style and harmony and grace and good rhythm depends on simplicity.

Plato,
Greek philosopher,
428–347 BCE

269

I tried to discover, in the rumor of forests and waves, words that other men could not hear, and I pricked up my ears to listen to the revelation of their harmony.

Gustave Flaubert,
French novelist,
1821–1880
trans. Juliet Herbert, 1862

GRATITUDE
AUTUMN–WINTER

Gratitude is a great attribute (almost a grace in itself) which is shared by both human beings and animals as a form of saying thank you. A simple act of thankfulness can turn a stranger into a friend and strengthens the bonds between man and nature. Even animals have been observed to reciprocate with gratitude as a form of acknowledgement, after receiving care from another.

The act of gratitude has been described as the backbone of human society; it has been compared to a science and studied by historians and psychologists from every point of view. Is gratitude an emotion, is it a virtue? Is it natural, or is it cultivated? Does it involve everyone, or is it something that we can only truly express to a god?

Neuroscientists have identified areas in the brain that are likely involved in the expression of gratitude. Other studies have found additional evidence that identifies certain genes which respond positively to the experience of gratitude.

Connected to the natural response to say a simple thank you is a very conscious decision to offer thanks for something that benefits more than one person. Thanksgiving is often the term used while we share our gratitude together for the food that is placed before us. Peoples from all over the world, from time immemorial, have given thanks to the sun and to the rain, to the gods and to each other, for what they are about to receive. Sometimes this is also referred to as "grace", which can take the form of a prayer to be said when all the nourishment presented on a table is attributed to the goodness of either Mother Nature or a god.

The idea of grace is very similar to the idea of harmony. It cannot exist by itself, as it must come from somewhere, comprised of gesture and acknowledgement, as in clouds and rain, and bees and honey. It relies on the fusion of other elements, but these are not always as tangible. Grace can be a gift from god, but it can also be associated and adapted to describe anything from the way a swimmer glides through the water, to a beautifully created piece of cloth which moves gracefully. Here, "grace" becomes an elegance, and a sophistication:

> Whenas in silks my Julia goes,
> Then, then (methinks) how sweetly flows
> The liquefaction of her clothes.
>
> > Robert Herrick (1591–1674),
> > from "Upon Julia's Clothes"

Sadly, there can also be deeply ingrained resistance to the emotive qualities of gratitude, thanksgiving and grace which are often associated with envy, materialism, narcissism and cynicism. However, saying thank you and showing gratitude is not demeaning; to admit indebtedness is not weakness, it could even be deemed a grace.

The wise old world of words records people offering words of thanksgiving to express their gratitude by saying thank you for many, many different reasons. Gratitude creates a special bond between the world and our place within it. A nod, a bow, a smile or a touch will often pass for an acknowledgement of thanks. More than anything, though, it is a sign of sharing, of kindness, and is characterized by a universal set of gestures.

There are many ways to express gratitude, and they are worth trying, most are subtle and don't involve words.

- ❖ Gratitude can be expressed by listening intently to someone as they share a story.

- ❖ A nod can connect two strangers when one has helped the other.

- ❖ A flash of car headlights can thank an oncoming driver for their forethought.

- ❖ Two hands, palms pressed lightly together, is a universal sign of gratitude and of grace.

- ❖ A flower offered to someone suggests a thanking of some sort.

The benefits of remembering to thank someone, or offering a word of gratitude to the heavens, have long been known to help with cherishing inner peace and restoring inner harmony.

QUESTIONS TO REFLECT ON

- ❖ Do you think that a more universal sense of thanks could change the world from being a selfish, ego-centred place to one of greater equanimity among all nations?

- ❖ How good are you at saying thank you?

- ❖ How do you feel when somebody thanks you?

- ❖ Do you think that an act of gratitude is a positive way of creating a special link between two sentient beings, patting the head of a dog, stroking a sweet-natured cat?

The more grateful you are, the more present you become.

270

I would maintain that thanks are the highest form of thought; and that gratitude is happiness doubled by wonder.

G. K. Chesterton,
English writer,
1874–1936

271

Wear gratitude like a cloak and it will feed every corner of your life.

Rumi,
Persian poet and mystic,
1207–1273

272

I can no other answer make
But thanks, and thanks and
ever thanks.

William Shakespeare,
English playwright,
1564–1616
From *Twelfth Night*, Act III Scene 3

273

Appreciation is a wonderful thing: it makes what is excellent in others belong to us as well.

Voltaire,
French Enlightenment writer,
1694–1778

274

Hem your blessings with
thankfulness so they don't
unravel.

Anonymous

275

Forgiveness is the fragrance that the violet sheds on the heel that crushed it.

Mark Twain,
American writer and novelist,
1835–1910

Some folk hae meat and canna eat,
And some wad eat that want it;
But we hae meat, and we can eat,
And say the Lord be thankit.

Attributed to Robert Burns,
Scottish poet and lyricist,
1759–1796
"The Selkirk Grace"

277

Be Grateful
For your Life …
Every detail of it …
And your face will come to shine like
 the sun …
And everyone who sees it …
Will be made glad and peaceful.

Rumi,
Persian poet and mystic,
1207–1273

278

Full many a blessing wears this guise
Of worry or of trouble.
Farseeing is the soul and wise
Who knows the mask is double.
But he who has the faith and strength
To thank his God for sorrow
Has found a joy without alloy
To gladden every morrow.

We ought to make the moments notes
Of happy, glad Thanksgiving;
The hours and days a silent phase
Of music we are living.
And so the theme should swell and grow
As weeks and months pass o'er us,
And rise sublime at this good time,
A grand Thanksgiving chorus.

Ella Wheeler Wilcox,
American author and poet,
1850–1919
From "Thanksgiving"

279

Count your blessings instead of your crosses; count your gains instead of your losses.

Anonymous

280

In other gardens
And all up the vale,
From autumn bonfires
See the smoke trail!

Pleasant summer over,
And all the summer flowers,
The red fire blazes,
The grey smoke towers.

Sing a song of seasons!
Something bright in all!
Flowers in the summer,
Fires in the fall!

Robert Lewis Stevenson,
Scottish novelist, poet and travel writer,
1850–1894
"Autumn Fires"

281

O! Lord make us able
For all on the table.

Anonymous, Irish "grace" often said
by just the children at the table

282

Bless us, O Lord,
And these, Thy gifts
Which we are about to receive,
From Thy bounty.
Through Christ, Our Lord,
Amen.

Christian Mass blessing

283

I thank thee God, that I have lived
In this great world and known its many joys:
The songs of birds, the strongest sweet scent of
   hay,
And cooling breezes in the secret dusk:
The flaming sunsets at the close of day,
Hills and the lovely, heather-covered moors;
Music at night, and the moonlight on the sea,
The beat of waves upon the rocky shore
And wild white spray, flung high in ecstasy;
The faithful eyes of dogs, and treasured books,
The love of Kin and fellowship of friends
And all that makes life dear and beautiful.

Elizabeth Craven, Baroness Craven,
English writer,
1750–1826
From "I Thank Thee God, That I Have Lived"

284

He is a wise man who does not grieve for the things which he has not, but rejoices in those which he has.

Epictetus,
Greek Stoic philosopher,
55–135 CE

285

Let us be grateful to people who make us happy; they are the charming gardeners who make our souls blossom.

Marcel Proust,
French novelist,
1871–1922

286

Gratitude turns what we have into enough.

Anonymous

287

Gratitude is not only the greatest of virtues but the parent of all others.

Cicero,
Roman statesman,
106–43 BCE

288

You cannot do a kindness too soon because you never know how soon it will be too late.

Ralph Waldo Emerson,
American essayist and poet,
1803–1882

289

Nothing is more honourable then a grateful heart.

Seneca,
Roman Stoic philosopher,
4 BCE–65 CE

290

Lord, thou hast given me a cell,
Wherein to dwell;
A little house, whose humble roof
Is weather proof;
Under the spars of which I lie
Both soft and dry;
Where thou, my chamber for to ward,
Hast set a guard
Of harmless thoughts, to watch and keep
Me, while I sleep.

Robert Herrick,
English lyric poet and cleric,
1591–1674
From "A Thanksgiving to God"

291

Nothing more detestable does the earth produce then an ungrateful man.

Decimus Magnus Ausonius,
Roman poet and teacher,
310–395 CE

292

What if the little rain should say,
"So small a drop as I
Can ne'er refresh the thirsty earth,
I'll tarry in the sky!"

What if the shining beam of noon
Should in its fountain stay,
Because its feeble light alone
Is not enough for day!

Doth not each rain-drop help to form
The cool refreshing shower?
And every ray of light to warm
And beautify the flower?

William Cutter,
American poet,
1801–1867
"The Value of Little Things"

293

Today I choose to live with gratitude for the love that fills my heart, the peace that rests within my spirit, and the voice of hope that says all things are possible.

Anonymous

294

Gratitude is the sign of noble souls.

Aesop,
Greek fabulist and storyteller,
c.620–564 BCE

295

If the only prayer you said was thank you, that would be enough.

Meister Eckhart,
German theologian, philosopher and mystic,
1260–1328

296

… gratitude is a shortcut
which speedily leads to love.

Théophile Gautier,
French poet, dramatist and novelist,
1811–1872
From "Madame de Maupin"

297

A thankful heart is a happy heart.

Anonymous

298

Life, if well lived, is long enough. Every new beginning comes from some other beginning's end.

The greatest blessings of mankind are within us and within our reach. A wise man is content with his lot, whatever it may be, without wishing for what he has not.

Seneca,
Roman Stoic philosopher,
4 BCE–65 CE
trans. Thomas Morell, 1786

299

When eating bamboo sprouts, remember the man who planted them.

Chinese proverb

300

He who is not contented with what he has, would not be contented with what he would like to have.

Socrates,
Greek philosopher, founder of Western philosophy,
470–399 BCE

301

Forget injuries, but never forget kindness.

Confucius,
Chinese philosopher,
551–479 BCE

302

Whatever I am offered in devotion with a pure heart – a leaf, a flower, fruit, or water – I accept with joy.

From *Bhagavad Gita*

303

If you look to others for fulfilment you will never be fulfilled. If your happiness depends on money, you will never be happy with yourself. Be content with what you have; rejoice in the way things are when you realize there is nothing lacking, the world belongs to you.

Lao Tzu,
Chinese philosopher and writer,
6th/4th century BCE
trans. Thomas Wade, 1868

304

Do not tell the man that is carrying you that he stinks.

African proverb

305

Revenge is profitable,
gratitude is expensive.

Edward Gibbon,
English historian and writer,
1737–1794

306

If you cannot be grateful for what you have received, then be thankful for what you have been spared.

Yiddish saying

307

For grace is given not because we have done good works, but in order that we may be able to do them.

Saint Augustine,
Roman African theologian and philosopher,
354–430 CE

308

Amazing grace! (how sweet the
  sound)
That sav'd a wretch like me!
I once was lost, but now am found,
Was blind, but now I see.

John Newton,
English writer and hymn-writer,
1725–1807
From "Amazing Grace" (hymn)

309

I've heard of hearts unkind;
  kind deeds
With coldness still returning;
Alas! The gratitude of men
Hath oftener left me
  mourning.

William Wordsworth,
English Romantic poet,
1770–1850
From "Simon Lee: The Old Huntsman"

310

There is no knowledge so hard to acquire as to how to live this life well and naturally.

Michel de Montaigne,
French Renaissance philosopher and essayist,
1533–1592

311

God, I thank thee, that I am not as other men are.

New Testament, Matthew Ib. 11

312

How do I love thee? Let me count the
   ways.
I love thee to the depth and breadth
   and height
My soul can reach, when feeling out of
   sight
For the ends of Being and ideal Grace.

Elizabeth Barrett Browning,
English poet,
1806–1861

313

Who is this? And what is here?
And in the lighted palace near
Died the sound of royal cheer;
And they cross'd themselves for fear,
All the knights of Camelot:
But Lancelot mused a little space;
He said, "She has a lovely face;
God in his mercy lend her grace,
The Lady of Shalott."

Alfred, Lord Tennyson,
English poet,
1809–1892
From "The Lady of Shalott"

314

Monday's child is fair of face,
Tuesday's child is full of grace,
Wednesday's child is full of woe,
Thursday's child has far to go,
Friday's child is loving and giving,
Saturday's child works hard for a living,
And the child that is born in the
   Sabbath day
Is fair, and wise, and good and gay.

Nursery rhyme, first quoted in
A. E. Bray, *Traditions of Devonshire*

315

No Spring, nor Summer
  beauty hath such grace
As I have seen in one
  Autumnal face.

John Donne,
English poet,
1571–1631

316

No duty is more urgent than that of returning thanks.

Anonymous

317

Take full account of the excellencies which you possess, and in gratitude remember how you hanker after them, if you had them not.

Marcus Aurelius,
Roman emperor and Stoic philosopher,
121–180 CE

318

Thou that has given so much to me,
Give one more thing – a grateful heart;
Not thankful when it pleaseth me,
As if thy blessings had spare days;
But such a heart,
Whose pulse may be Thy praise.

George Herbert,
Welsh poet,
1593–1633

ENDINGS
WINTER

It is normal to think about endings. They are the inevitable conclusions to life events and can have the most profound emotional effect on us.

Everything that we do has a beginning and an ending. We are a part of these processes and contribute to them in some way from the moment we are born to the moment when we cross the threshold of death. During this time we will experience many types of endings, from glorious sunsets, to the sad glance at an empty bowl once overflowing with strawberries. Endings can be happy, or they can be heart-breaking; they might be the last fall of snow, or the sound of the bell at the end of a lesson. They may be the punch-line of a joke or the final words in a book, a diminuendo, a fading or a "drench of sleep", as Dorothy Wordsworth recalls in her Grasmere diaries. Endings leave memories engraved on your mind. The last line of Louisa May Alcott's masterpiece *Little Women* has a poignancy that touches on the past, present and future in just a few words: "Oh, my girls, however long you may live, I never can wish you a greater happiness than this!"

One inexhaustible, eternal question remains, however, and that is about the mystery of death. To this "end", poets and prayer-makers, thinkers and sages have raised their pens to ink their way into the dark unknown. In reality no one knows what lies beyond, but that has never prevented a curious mind from unleashing its imagination. Is the end the moment when we join those loved ones who have gone before us? Could our last breath be that glorious "release" from all human responsibility? Death, endings and the finality of a living organism have always intrigued mankind.

Endings need not only be about sad things like personal loss or tragedy; they can be about achievement, about freedom and release. They can be jubilant celebrations, like welcoming in the New Year; they can be the vote that changes a situation dramatically, or they can be the relief breathed at the end of a long journey. Perhaps their role in our lives becomes a marker of sorts for the moment when we could take a different road, change direction or find another way of doing something. They may even be as simple and fulfilling as watching the dawn rise over the rooftops, as the darkness ebbs away, as stealthy as a black cat leaving by the back door.

There are ways to help an ending be a good one. Here are a few ideas practised worldwide and from the moment time began:

❖ Remember to give thanks for all that is good.

❖ Try to love who you are, and remember that you are loved.

❖ Forgive all those who have hurt you, for the pain you bear is yours and yours alone.

❖ Endings are not about failure or the inability to survive; they are about transformation.

QUESTIONS TO REFLECT ON

❖ Are endings "absolute" in your world?

❖ Is there any such thing as a "happy ending"?

❖ How many different types of endings can you recall?

❖ Some people see an ending as the beginning of something new. Can you?

Every book is a quotation; and every house is a quotation made out of all forests, and mines, and stone quarries; and every man is a quotation from all his ancestors.

Ralph Waldo Emerson,
American philosopher (1803–1882)

Every ending is a new beginning.

319

People will not look forward to prosterity, who never look backward to their ancestors.

Edmund Burke,
Irish statesman and philosopher,
1729–1797

320

There's rosemary,
That's for remembrance;
Pray, love, remember:
and there is pansies, that's for thoughts.

William Shakespeare,
English playwright,
1564–1616
From *Hamlet*, Act IV Scene 5

321

Poetry should surprise by fine excess, and not by singularity; it should strike the reader as a wording of his own highest thoughts, and appear almost a remembrance.

John Keats,
English Romantic poet,
1795–1821
Letter to John Taylor, 1818

322

Please to remember
The Fifth of November,
Gunpowder treason and plot;
We know no reason
Why gunpowder treason
Should ever be forgot.

Anonymous nursery rhyme

323

Better by far you should forget and smile
Then that you should remember and be sad.

Christina Rossetti,
English poet,
1830–1894
From "Remember"

324

In the gloaming, O, my darling!
When the lights are dim and
  low,
And the quiet shadows falling,
Softly come and go.

Meta Orred,
English poet,
1845–1925
From "In the Gloaming"

325

There's a Friend for little
  children
Above the bright blue sky,
A Friend who never changes,
Whose love will never die.

Albert Midlane,
English poet and hymn-writer,
1825–1909
From "There's a Friend For Little Children"

326

Enough is as good as a feast.

Sir Thomas Mallory,
English writer,
c.1415–1471.

327

Youth, what man's age is like to be doth show;
We may our ends by our beginnings know.

Sir John Denham,
Anglo-Irish poet,
1615–1669
From "Of Prudence"

328

Softly sweet, in Lydian measures,
Soon he sooth'd his soul to pleasures.
War, he sung, is toil and trouble;
Honour but an empty bubble.
Never ending, still beginning,
Fighting still, and still destroying;
If the world be worth thy winning,
Think, O think, it worth enjoying:
Lovely Thais sits beside thee,
Take the good the gods provide thee.

John Dryden,
English literary critic, translator,
playwright and first Poet Laureate,
1631–1700
From "Alexander's Feast"

329

The head that once was
crowned with thorns
Is crowned with glory now.

Thomas Kelly,
Irish poet and hymn-writer,
1769–1854

330

If, when hearing that I have been stilled at last,
   they stand at the door,
Watching the full-starred heavens that winter sees,
Will this thought rise on those who will meet my
   face no more,
"He was one who had an eye for such mysteries"?

And will any say when the bell of quittance is
   heard in the gloom,
And the crossing breeze cuts a pause in its
   outrollings,
Till they rise again, as they were a new bell's boom,
"He hears it not now, but used to notice such
   things"?

Thomas Hardy,
English novelist and poet,
1840–1928
From "Afterwards"

331

Glory to God for dappled things –
For skies of couple-colour as a brinded cow;
For rose-moles all in stipple upon trout that swim;
Fresh-firecoal chestnut-falls; finches' wings;
Landscape plotted and pieced – fold, fallow, and
   plough;
And áll trádes, their gear and tackle and trim.

All things counter, original, spare, strange;
Whatever is fickle, freckled (who knows how?)
With swift, slow, sweet, sour; adazzle, dim;
He fathers-forth whose beauty is past change:
Praise him.

Gerard Manely Hopkins,
English poet and Jesuit priest,
1844–1889
"Pied Beauty"

332

I know that the day will come
When my sight of the earth shall be lost,
And life will take its leave in silence,
Drawing the last curtain over my eyes.

Yet stars will watch at night
And morning fire as before,
And hours heave like sea waves casting up
    pleasures and pains.

When I think of this end of my moments,
The barrier of the moments breaks
And I see by the light of death
Thy world with its careless treasures.
Rare is the lowliest seat,
Rare is its meanest of lives.

Things that I longed for in vain
And things that I got
– let them pass.
Let me but truly possess
the things that I ever spurned
and overlooked.

Rabindranath Tagore,
Bengali poet,
1861–1941
"Last Curtain"
trans. Subhas Dasgupta

333

New beginnings are often
disguised as painful endings.

Lao Tzu,
Chinese philosopher and writer,
6th/4th century BCE

334

To forget one's ancestors is to be a brook without a source, a tree without a root.

Chinese proverb

335

You are never alone, even during what you think are your weakest moments. You have thousands of years of powerful ANCESTORS within you, the blood of the Divine, Great Ones in you, supreme intellect and royalty in you. Infinite strength is always on tap for you. Know that.

Anonymous

336

What can be said in New Year rhymes,
That's not been said a thousand times?

The new years come, the old years go,
We know we dream, we dream we know.

We rise up laughing with the light,
We lie down weeping with the night.

We hug the world until it stings,
We curse it then and sigh for wings.

We live, we love, we woo, we wed,
We wreathe our brides, we sheet our dead.

We laugh, we weep, we hope we fear,
And that's the burden of a year.

Ella Wheeler Wilcox,
American author and poet,
1850–1919
"The Year"

337

Listen …
With faint dry sound,
Like steps of passing ghosts,
The leaves, frost-crisped, break from
   the trees
And fall.

Adelaide Crapsey,
American poet,
1878–1914
"November Night"

338

Open your ears to the ancestors and you will understand the language of the spirits.

African Proverb

339

Every action has an ancestor of a thought.

Ralph Waldo Emerson,
American essayist and poet,
1803–1882

340

Man's schemes are inferior to those made in heaven.

Chinese Proverb

341

When the grandmothers
speak, the earth will be healed.

Hopi proverb

342

All men's souls are immortal,
but the souls of the righteous
are divine.

Socrates,
Greek philosopher, founder of Western philosophy,
470–399 BCE

343

We do not inherit the earth from our ancestors, we borrow it from our children.

Native American proverb

344

"I keep turning over new leaves, and spoiling them, as I used to spoil my copy-books; and I make so many beginnings there never will be an end," he said, dolefully.

Louise May Alcott,
American novelist and poet,
1832–1888
From *Little Women*

345

Every day is a journey, and the journey itself is home.

Matsuo Bashō,
Japanese poet,
1644–1694

346

To finish the moment, to find the journeys end in every step of the road, to live the greatest number of good hours is wisdom.

Ralph Waldo Emerson,
American essayist and poet,
1803–1882

347

The years seem to rush by now, and I think of death as a fast approaching end, of a journey – double and treble reason for loving as well as working.

George Eliot, pen name of Mary Ann Evans, English novelist, poet, journalist and translator, 1819–1880

348

To be an ancestoral believer is to be a good ancestor.

African Proverb

349

Long journeys are strange things: if we were always to continue in the same mind we are in at the end of a journey, we should never stir from the place we were then in: but Providence in kindness to us causes us to forget it. It is much the same with lying-in women. Heaven permits this forgetfulness that the world is peopled, and that folks take journeys to Provance.

Marie de Rabutin-Chantel,
marquise of Sévigné,
French author,
1626-1696
trans. M Gualt de Saint Benedict

350

I wish you to know that you have been the last dream of my soul.

Charles Dickens,
English writer and social critic,
1812–1879
From *A Tale of Two Cities*

351

I do not fear death. I had been dead for billions and billions of years before I was born, and had not suffered the slightest inconvenience from it.

Mark Twain,
American writer and novelist,
1835–1910

352

Goodbyes are only for those who love with their eyes. Because for those who loved with heart and soul, there is no separation.

Rumi,
Persian poet and mystic,
1207–1273

353

Such wilt thou be to me, who must,
Like th'other foot, obliquely run;
Thy firmness makes my circle just,
And makes me end where I begun.

John Donne,
English poet,
1571–1631
From "A Valediction"

354

This World is not Conclusion.
A Species stands beyond –
Invisible, as Music –
But positive, as Sound.

Emily Dickinson,
American poet,
1830–1886
From "This World Is Not Conclusion"

355

Here lies a poor woman who always was tired,
For she lived in a place where help wasn't hired.
Her last words on earth were, Dear friends I am
   going
Where washing ain't done nor sweeping nor
   sewing,
And everything there is exact to my wishes,
For there they don't eat and there's no washing of
   dishes,
Don't mourn for me now, don't mourn for me
   never,
For I'm going to do nothing for ever and ever.

Epitaph in Bushy Churchyard, 1860,
destroyed 1916. Quoted in a letter
to the *Spectator*, 2 September 1922

356

God be in my head,
And in my understanding;

God be in my eyes,
And in my looking;

God be in my mouth,
And in my speaking;

God be in my heart,
And in my thinking;

God be at my end,
And at my departing.

Sarum Missal, 1007 CE

357

Creep into thy narrow bed,
Creep, and let no more be said!
Vain thy onset! all stands fast
Thou thyself must break at last.

Let the long contention cease!
Geese are swans, and swans are geese.
Let them have it how they will!
Thou art tired; best be still.

Matthew Arnold,
English poet,
1822–1888
From "The Last Word"

358

Don't grieve. Anything that you lose comes around in another form.

Rumi,
Persian poet and mystic,
1207–1273

359

He who binds to himself a joy
Doth the winged life destroy;
He who kisses the joy as it flies
Lives in eternity's sun rise.

William Blake,
English poet, painter and printmaker,
1757–1827
"Eternity"

360

Since there's no help, come let us kiss and part
Nay, I have done, you get no more of me;
And I am glad, yea glad with all my heart
That thus so cleanly I myself can free.
Shake hands for ever, cancel all our vows,
And when we meet at any time again,
Be it not seen in either of our brows
That we one jot of former love retain.

Michael Drayton,
English poet,
1563–1631
From "Since There's No Help"

361

Time goes a running, even as
  we talk.
Take the present, the future's
  no one's affair

Horace,
Roman lyric poet,
65 BCE–8 BCE
From "Ode 1.11"

362

Whenever you see a hearse go by
And think to yourself that you're gonna die,
Be merry, my friends, be merry

They put you in a big white shirt
And cover you over with tons of dirt,
Be merry, my friend, be merry.

They put you in a long-shaped box
And cover you over with tons of rocks,
Be merry, my friends, be merry.

The worms crawl out and the worms crawl in,
The ones that crawl in are lean and thin,
The ones that crawl out are fat and stout,
Be merry, my friend, be merry.

Your eyes fall in and your hair falls out
And your brains come tumbling down your snout,
Be merry, my friends, be merry.

Anonymous
"Be Merry"

363

Time is a sort of river of passing events, and strong is its current; no sooner is a thing brought to sight then it is swept by and another takes its place, and this too will be swept away.

Marcus Aurelius,
Roman emperor and Stoic philosopher,
121–180 CE

364

Wae's me, wae's me,
The acorn's not yet
Fallen from the tree
That's to grow the wood,
That's to make the cradle,
That's to rock the bairn,
That's to grow the man,
That's to lay me.

Anonomous
"The Wandering Spectre"

365

I am the family face;
Flesh perishes I live on,
Projecting trait and trace
Through time to time anon,
And leaping from place to place over oblivion.
The years-heired feature that can
In curve and voice and eye
Despise the human span
Of durance – that is I;
The eternal thing in man,
That heeds no call to die.

Thomas Hardy,
English novelist and poet,
1840–1928
"Heredity"

AFTERWORD

At the start of this collection, the path towards this final group of sayings and poems led the reader from spring and the beginnings, through the magical process of purification, towards renewal. Summer dawns and a time of abundance turns into richness and prosperity, when the harmonies of sun and moon maintain a careful balance. As we harvest the goodness brought on by all that has passed from the beginnings of the year, the ending looms with the onset of winter, when the sun will set and we assume that darkness will ensue. Everything, however, begins again, as the immutable engine of life rolls back the hours and produces more and more time.

It could almost be that there has never been such things as a "real" beginning or a genuine ending ... maybe it is all just a gentle ebb and flow of ceaseless wonder.

In the wise and gentle words of Michel de Montaigne, the French Renaissance philosopher: "Rejoice in the present; all else is beyond thee."

ABOUT TRIGGER PUBLISHING

Trigger is a leading independent altruistic global publisher devoted to opening up conversations about mental health and wellbeing. We share uplifting and inspirational mental health stories, publish advice-driven books by highly qualified clinicians for those in recovery and produce wellbeing books that will help you to live your life with greater meaning and clarity. We want to help you to not just survive but thrive … one book at a time.

Find out more about Trigger Publishing by visiting our website: triggerpublishing.com or join us on:

Twitter @TriggerPub
Facebook @TriggerPub
Instagram @TriggerPub

ABOUT SHAWMIND

A proportion of profits from the sale of all Trigger books go to their sister charity, Shawmind. The charity aims to ensure that everyone has access to mental health resources whenever they need them.

shawmind.org
Twitter @Shaw_Mind
Facebook @shawmindUK
Instagram @Shaw_Mind